Promoting University-Industry Collaboration in Sri Lanka

**DIRECTIONS IN DEVELOPMENT**
Human Development

# Promoting University-Industry Collaboration in Sri Lanka

*Status, Case Studies, and Policy Options*

Kurt Larsen, Deepthi C. Bandara, Mohamed Esham, and Ranmini Unantenne

 **WORLD BANK GROUP**

# Contents

## Boxes

## Figures

## Tables

# Acknowledgments

This study was carried out by a team consisting of Professor Deepthi Bandara, Deputy Project Director of the Higher Education for the Twenty First Century (HETC) Project and Director of the Quality Assurance and Accreditation Council of the University Grants Commission; Ranmini Unantenne, Manager of Career Guidance at the Sri Lanka Institute of Information Technology and former Project Officer in the Policy Planning and Development Unit of the HETC Project; and Kurt Larsen, Senior Education Specialist at the World Bank. Mohamed Esham of Sabaragamuwa University was engaged as a consultant to carry out the survey on university-industry collaboration and analyze the survey results. Technical support for the survey was provided by Mr. Nuwan Seneviratne and Mr. Naveen Muthukumarana of the HETC Project.

The team expresses its gratitude to the university faculty and company staff who took their valuable time to respond to the survey questionnaires. Their insights and willingness to share information and experiences were essential to the study's success. Special thanks go to the faculty who drafted the collaboration case studies in appendix A. The following peer reviewers provided many valuable suggestions and comments on the report: Professor Ajith de Alwis, University of Moratuwa; Professor Sarath Kodithuwakku, University of Peradeniya; Ananda Assiriyage, CIC CropGuard Pvt. Ltd.; Javier Botero Alvarez, Senior Education Specialist, World Bank; and Roberta Bassett, Senior Education Specialist, World Bank. The team also thanks colleagues who have been very supportive throughout the process of drafting this report, including Professor P. S. M. Gunaratne, Acting Director of the HETC Project and Vice-Chairman of the University Grants Commission; D. H. C. Aturupane, Lead Education Specialist, World Bank; Yoko Nagashima, Senior Education Specialist, World Bank; and Benoit Millot, Higher Education Specialist and consultant, World Bank. Finally, the team also thanks the World Bank's Publishing and Knowledge Division and Catherine Sunshine, who did an excellent job of editing the report.

# About the Authors

**Deepthi C. Bandara** (PhD, Pennsylvania State University, USA) is a senior professor at the University of Peradeniya, Sri Lanka. An agricultural biologist, she has been actively engaged in teaching methodology, curriculum development, quality assurance, and staff development, in addition to her own teaching and research. She has been a consultant on World Bank–assisted projects on higher education in Sri Lanka over the past 12 years, working on innovations in teaching, learning, and assessment, and fostering university-industry partnerships for commercialization and dissemination of research. She also serves as director of the Quality Assurance and Accreditation Council of the University Grants Commission in Sri Lanka.

**Mohamed Esham** (PhD, Tottori University, Japan) is a professor of agribusiness management at Sabaragamuwa University of Sri Lanka, with two decades of experience as an academic and researcher. His research interests include climate change adaptation, food security, farmer-based organizations, entrepreneurship, and entrepreneurial universities. He has published numerous articles on issues related to economics of smallholder agriculture, climate change, and university-industry collaboration. He has received a number of international awards and fellowships, including the Commonwealth Academic Fellowship, Japan Foundation Fellowship, Australian Endeavour Fellowship, and the Experts for Asia award from the European Union.

**Kurt Larsen** (MPA, École Nationale d'Administration, Paris, and MSc, Aarhus University, Denmark) has worked for the World Bank since 2005 as a senior education specialist. He joined the South Asia Education Team in 2011 and works on higher education projects in India, Sri Lanka, and Afghanistan. Previously he led the Knowledge for Development Program at the World Bank Institute. Before joining the Bank, he was a senior analyst in the Education Directorate of the Organisation for Economic Co-operation and Development (OECD), where he conducted policy research on education and science and technology development. He worked for more than 10 years in the Danish Ministry of Education, Ministry of Science and Technology, and Prime Minister's Office. He is the author of several books and reports on higher education, innovation, and the knowledge economy.

**Ranmini Unantenne** (MSc, University of Peradeniya, Sri Lanka) is manager of career guidance at the Sri Lanka Institute of Information Technology. She previously served as the project officer in charge of the Quality and Innovation Grant of the Higher Education for the Twenty First Century (HETC) Project, managing a competitively awarded grant scheme to improve teaching, learning, and research at state universities by providing additional resources. She has also worked with the International Water Management Institute, IRC Netherlands, and Stockholm Environment Institute in her career in the development sector.

# Executive Summary

Strong science, technology, and innovation links between universities and industry are of critical importance to Sri Lanka as it strives to become an upper-middle-income country. Sri Lanka's growth path will need to rely on knowledge-intensive activities such as information technology, engineering, industrial processing, and financial services. Closer collaboration between universities and companies in these activities is essential to improve corporate competitiveness and accelerate sustainable growth.

Historically, Sri Lankan universities have had a low level of research and development (R&D) activity, as the prime duty of their faculty is teaching. At the same time, companies in Sri Lanka do not have a significant record of R&D expenditures, absorption of new technologies, or innovation measured in terms of patents issued. There is a strategic need to promote research, innovation, and technology development in order to increase the productivity and competitiveness of Sri Lanka's economy in agriculture, manufacturing, and services. Stronger university-industry (U-I) collaboration is an important component of such a strategy.

This report presents an overview of current U-I collaboration in Sri Lanka by analyzing responses to a survey of companies and university departments in 2015. Data from the 2015 survey are compared with data from a similar survey in 2007 to identify trends over time. The study examines current policies to promote U-I collaboration in Sri Lanka, highlights some good practices in other countries, and suggests possible ways that Sri Lanka may be able to strengthen U-I collaboration. The recommendations are intended primarily for policy makers in the fields of higher education, research, and innovation, as well as for researchers in companies, universities, and research institutes who are already collaborating in public-private partnerships or are planning to do so.

Two structured questionnaires were developed for the 2015 study, one for academia and one for industry. The study covered all 15 national universities, with responses from 165 academic departments, units, and centers. Seven major disciplines were represented: agriculture, arts, engineering, health sciences, information technology, management, and science. On the industry side, responses were received from 80 companies in the manufacturing, trading, services, construction, and information technology sectors, with the largest share of sampled firms involved in manufacturing. The majority of companies had more than 100 employees and annual turnover of more than SL Rs 500 million.

The responses show that the majority of existing links between Sri Lankan universities and companies are short-term, informal interactions with low direct transfer of knowledge and innovation. However, there are increasing examples of R&D partnerships between companies and universities in Sri Lanka that are strategic and long-lasting. Both companies and universities are aware of the importance of U-I collaboration and are increasingly willing to finance it. Overall, the percentage of university departments receiving external funding from any source has not changed significantly since 2007, but industry's share of such funding has increased. The survey findings also show a growing emphasis on deeper and more demanding types of collaboration, such as joint R&D activities, prototype testing, and spin-offs, even though these remain relatively uncommon.

University respondents cite lack of time to undertake industry-related research due to heavy academic workload, inadequate laboratory facilities and infrastructure, and lack of proper mechanisms to facilitate collaboration as major constraints on opportunities for joint work with industry. For companies, the predominant barrier appears to be the lack of proper mechanisms to facilitate collaboration with universities. Other constraints mentioned by industry respondents include a lack of entrepreneurial spirit among academics, the low commercialization potential of university research, incompatibility of university structures for collaboration, and lack of awareness of facilities and expertise available in universities.

To complement the analysis of survey findings, four case studies were developed by faculty at the Universities of Peradeniya, Colombo, Wayamba, and Moratuwa, presenting their institutions' experiences with U-I collaboration. These profiles, presented in an appendix, address the mutual advantages of collaboration, success factors, funding and operational models, implementation constraints, and barriers to sustainability.

Public policy can significantly influence U-I collaboration through various policy instruments, including (a) direct and indirect funding to universities and companies, such as R&D grant schemes and tax incentives; (b) regulatory measures that shape the rules for collaboration between universities and companies (for example, an intellectual property rights scheme); and (c) creation of intermediate organizations such as technology transfer offices and business incubators. Many of these policies have been embraced in Sri Lanka, but they have not always been fully implemented because of lack of funding and/or implementation capacity.

Recommendations for actions to strengthen U-I collaboration in Sri Lanka are based on the analysis of survey findings, on the case studies, and on discussions at a workshop on Promoting University-Industry Collaborations in Sri Lanka, held in Colombo in January 2016. They include possible policy reforms and other initiatives to be undertaken by government, universities, and companies. Among the key recommendations are the following:

- As part of the national Science, Technology, & Innovation Policy 2016–2020, develop and implement a forthcoming national plan to upgrade the country's research infrastructure, in line with national research and innovation priorities.
- Strengthen R&D funding schemes for joint projects between universities/ research institutes and companies, based on national and international experiences.
- Consider taking steps to modernize the existing University Act of 1978 and the financial management rules of universities to better facilitate U-I partnerships, consultancies, and education services.
- Define and implement clear intellectual property rights rules for publicly funded research to encourage the use of research results and ensure effective and timely legal protection of intellectual property.
- Establish open innovation spaces and business incubators at universities and make available seed money for faculty and students to develop start-ups.
- Strengthen the U-I interaction cells at universities with professional expertise in technology transfer and business model development.
- Establish opportunities for master's and PhD students to pursue targeted research projects in companies as part of their study.
- Facilitate mutual board memberships: universities can invite industry members to sit on university and faculty boards, and industry can invite faculty members to sit on company boards.
- Design and pilot a web-based database with reliable, useful, updated information about the current status of Sri Lanka's science, technology, and innovation activities.

# Abbreviations

| | |
|---|---|
| AFIS | Automated Fingerprint Identification System |
| COSTI | Coordinating Secretariat for Science, Technology and Innovation |
| CREST | Collaborative Research in Engineering, Science & Technology |
| CSC | Computing Services Centre |
| DAPH | Department of Animal Production and Health |
| DCPE | Department of Chemical and Process Engineering |
| DFST | Department of Food Science and Technology |
| FDI | foreign direct investment |
| FSQAL | Food Safety and Quality Assurance Laboratory |
| FVMAS | Faculty of Veterinary Medicine and Animal Science |
| GDP | gross domestic product |
| HETC | Higher Education for the Twenty First Century |
| IC | Innovation Center |
| ICT | information and communication technologies |
| ICTA | Information and Communication Technology Agency |
| IP | intellectual property |
| IPR | intellectual property rights |
| IRQUE | Improving Relevance and Quality of Undergraduate Education |
| IT | information technology |
| KTP | Knowledge Transfer Partnership |
| LAN | Lankan Angel Network |
| MOU | memorandum of understanding |
| NLDB | National Livestock Development Board |
| NRC | National Research Council of Sri Lanka |
| NSF | National Science Foundation of Sri Lanka |
| OECD | Organisation for Economic Co-operation and Development |
| PCT | Patent Cooperation Treaty |
| PRI | public research institute |
| R&D | research and development |

| | |
|---|---|
| SCOM | Samson Compounds Pvt. Ltd. |
| SL Rs | Sri Lanka rupees |
| SLIC | Sri Lanka Inventors Commission |
| SLINTEC | Sri Lanka Institute of Nanotechnology |
| SME | small and medium enterprise |
| TTO | technology transfer office |
| UCSC | University of Colombo School of Computing |
| UGC | University Grants Commission |
| U-I | university-industry |
| UNIC | Uni-Consultancy Services |
| UOC | University of Colombo |
| UOM | University of Moratuwa |
| VBC | Veterinary Business Center |
| WUSL | Wayamba University of Sri Lanka |

# Introduction

Strong science, technology, and innovation links between universities and industry are of critical importance to Sri Lanka as it strives to become an upper-middle-income country. Sri Lanka's growth path will need to rely on knowledge-intensive activities such as information technology, engineering, industrial processing, and financial services. Closer collaboration between universities and companies in these activities is essential to improve corporate competitiveness and accelerate sustainable growth.

The government of Sri Lanka is keen to promote university-industry (U-I) collaboration and partnerships. The Science, Technology & Innovation Strategy for Sri Lanka 2011–2015 as well as the corresponding National Coordinating and Monitoring Framework 2013–2015 stress the need to identify a national university-industry partnership policy as part of the overall governance of the innovation ecosystem in Sri Lanka.

It is in this context that the Policy Planning and Development Unit of the Higher Education for the Twenty First Century (HETC) Project in the Ministry of Higher Education and Highways, in partnership with the World Bank, decided to draft this report. The report has three main objectives:

- To describe and analyze the status and progress of U-I collaboration in Sri Lanka;
- To provide an overview of existing policies to promote U-I collaboration in Sri Lanka, as well as highlighting international good practices in fostering such collaboration; and
- To identify concrete ways forward to strengthen U-I collaboration in Sri Lanka.

Chapter 1 provides a brief overview of Sri Lanka's research and development (R&D) investments and innovation performance and reviews the different types of U-I collaboration. The team developed a survey to collect current data on U-I collaboration to address the first of the study objectives, with separate questionnaires for companies and university departments (appendix B). Based on key results of the 2015 survey, chapter 2 analyzes the status of U-I collaboration in Sri Lanka. A similar survey questionnaire was administered in 2007, allowing the current study team to compare U-I collaboration activities under way in 2015 with those in 2007 and identify major trends over time.

To complement the survey data, four case studies were developed by faculty at the Universities of Colombo, Moratuwa, Peradeniya, and Wayamba, presenting specific experiences with U-I collaboration at these universities. The profiles address issues such as the mutual advantages of collaboration, criteria for success, funding and operational models, sharing of experiences, constraints faced during implementation, and barriers to sustainability. The case studies are presented in appendix A.

Chapter 3 provides an overview of existing policies for promoting and regulating U-I collaboration in Sri Lanka and selected other countries. It also identifies some international good practices in promoting U-I collaboration.

Drawing on the findings in chapters 1–3 and on the case studies, chapter 4 suggests possible ways to strengthen U-I collaboration in Sri Lanka. These recommendations benefited greatly from a stakeholder workshop on Promoting University-Industry Collaborations in Sri Lanka that took place on January 19, 2016, in Colombo (appendix C). Opened by the Hon. Lakshman Kiriella, Minister of Higher Education and Highways, the workshop brought together participants from universities and industry as well as key policy makers from the Ministry of Higher Education and Highways, the University Grants Commission (UGC), the Coordinating Secretariat for Science, Technology and Innovation (COSTI), and other agencies. Participants developed a matrix of actions to be taken over the short and medium-to-long terms, with suggestions as to which organizations could be responsible for implementing the actions.

# CHAPTER 1

# Overview of University-Industry Collaboration in Sri Lanka

## Introduction

Collaboration between universities and industries is critical for relevant skills development through education and training; for the generation, acquisition, and adoption of knowledge through innovation and technology transfer; and for commercialization of research and promotion of entrepreneurship through start-up and spin-off companies (Guimón 2013).

Almost all industrial countries have moved over the last 10–20 years to make university-industry links a centerpiece of their innovation systems. Besides the developed countries, several developing countries such as China, India, Malaysia, and Singapore, among others, have introduced policies to promote stronger U-I collaboration. In particular, the drive for innovation and economic development in a knowledge society requires universities to play a more prominent role. If universities can significantly increase the flow of innovation through their own basic and applied research, and if such innovations can be applied in the business sector, the argument goes, countries with dynamic university sectors can count on higher rates of growth, especially if the benefits of new findings tend to remain localized for a period of time. University-industry collaboration can also increase the relevance of R&D investments and increase the mobility of labor between public and private sectors.

Government sometimes acts as a third partner in these undertakings. The concept of a "triple helix" has been used to represent a symbiotic relationship between government (central and local), universities, and the business community (Etzkowitz and Leydesdorff 1997). The triple helix thesis holds that contributions from universities, industry, and government can be combined to generate new institutional and social formats for the production, transfer, and application of knowledge.

## Sri Lanka's Research and Development Investments and Innovation Performance

To understand the context in which U-I collaboration takes place, it is useful to briefly review Sri Lanka's overall R&D and innovation activities. Sri Lanka spent a total of SL Rs 8,778.6 million (US$69.4 million) on R&D in 2010, which is the last year that R&D data were collected. This corresponds to 0.16 percent of the country's gross domestic product (GDP), which was a considerable increase over the amount spent in 2008 (0.11 percent). Sri Lanka spends less on R&D as a percentage of GDP than Thailand (0.21 percent) or Malaysia (0.64 percent), and significantly less than Singapore (2.43 percent), but more than the Philippines (0.11 percent). The business enterprise sector contribution to R&D expenditure increased to SL Rs 3,592.6 million in 2010, which was 41 percent of the total R&D expenditure and 0.06 percent of GDP.

Historically, Sri Lankan universities have had a low level of R&D activity, as the prime duty of their faculty is teaching. In 2010, only 11 percent of R&D expenditure was carried out by universities, compared with 45 percent by government research institutes and 44 percent by business enterprises. Over the last five years, however, greater emphasis has been placed on the need for university faculty to do research. Universities now require a PhD as a baseline credential for hiring, and faculty are asked to actively pursue both teaching and research in their academic careers. It is likely, therefore, that R&D expenditures at universities currently account for more than 11 percent of total R&D expenditure in Sri Lanka.

At the same time, companies in Sri Lanka do not have a significant record of R&D expenditures, absorption of new technologies, or innovation measured in terms of the number of patents issued. This might be one of the factors that explains Sri Lanka's steady decline in the trade of goods and services as a percentage of GDP, which was 89 percent in 2000 but decreased to 54 percent in 2013. Investments in R&D, and the quality of R&D activities, have been insufficient to ensure effective modernization of agriculture and the food manufacturing industry. Indeed, the percentage of the agriculture budget allocated to R&D and extension is smaller in Sri Lanka than in other Asian countries (World Bank 2015).

Based on rankings from the World Economic Forum, Sri Lanka performs less well than comparable countries in the absorption of existing technologies that are new to the country, in firm-level technology absorption, and in attracting technology through foreign direct investment (FDI) as a way to enhance the productivity of existing industries (table 1.1).

In terms of the perceived quality of research institutions in the country, Sri Lanka is doing relatively well, as it is ranked number 47 out of 144 economies in the World Economic Forum's survey (table 1.2). On the other hand, Sri Lanka's ranking on U-I collaboration, which is the topic of this report, is much less favorable, with only Bangladesh among nine comparator countries doing worse. Sri Lanka also has a mediocre ranking on the number of parent

**Table 1.1  Technology Readiness Ranking, Sri Lanka and Comparators, 2014–15**

| Country | Availability of latest technologies | Firm-level technology absorption | FDI and technology transfer |
|---|---|---|---|
| Bangladesh | 99 | 108 | 112 |
| Indonesia | 53 | 42 | 40 |
| Malaysia | 33 | 24 | 8 |
| Mauritius | 48 | 44 | 57 |
| Philippines | 58 | 41 | 31 |
| Singapore | 15 | 16 | 2 |
| **Sri Lanka** | **70** | **53** | **53** |
| Thailand | 74 | 55 | 15 |
| Vietnam | 123 | 121 | 93 |

*Source:* World Economic Forum 2014.
*Note:* The value for each indicator is the country's ranking out of 144 economies; lower numbers indicate better performance. Rankings are based on three questions from the World Economic Forum's Executive Opinion Survey for 2014: (a) In your country, to what extent are the latest technologies available? (b) To what extent do businesses in your country absorb new technology? (c) To what extent does foreign direct investment bring new technology into your country?

**Table 1.2  Innovation Ranking, Sri Lanka and Comparators, 2014–15**

| Country | Quality of scientific research institutions | U-I collaboration | PCT patent applications |
|---|---|---|---|
| Bangladesh | 122 | 132 | 120 |
| Indonesia | 41 | 30 | 106 |
| Malaysia | 20 | 12 | 32 |
| Mauritius | 91 | 101 | 86 |
| Philippines | 75 | 55 | 31 |
| Singapore | 11 | 5 | 13 |
| **Sri Lanka** | **47** | **110** | **76** |
| Thailand | 61 | 46 | 67 |
| Vietnam | 96 | 92 | 93 |

*Source:* World Economic Forum 2014.
*Note:* The value for each indicator is the country's ranking out of 144 economies; lower numbers indicate better performance. Rankings in columns 1 and 2 are based on two questions from the World Economic Forum's Executive Opinion Survey for 2014: (a) In your country, how do you assess the quality of scientific research institutions? and (b) In your country, to what extent do people collaborate and share ideas between companies and universities/research institutions? Rankings in column 3 are based on the number of patent applications filed under the PCT per million population.

applications filed under the Patent Cooperation Treaty (PCT). The PCT makes it possible to seek patent protection for an invention simultaneously in a large number of countries by filing a single "international" patent application instead of filing several separate national or regional applications.

These indicators illustrate the strategic need to promote research, innovation, and technology development in order to increase the productivity and competitiveness of Sri Lanka's economy in agriculture, manufacturing, and services. Stronger U-I collaboration is an important component of such a strategy.

Promoting University-Industry Collaboration in Sri Lanka  •  http://dx.doi.org/10.1596/978-1-4648-0922-4

## Types of University-Industry Collaboration

There are many different forms of university-industry collaboration. They range from interactions that are mainly informal and low-intensity, such as participation in social networks and joint meetings, workshops, or training activities, to robust and intensive partnerships, such as pursuing joint R&D projects together. It is also useful to distinguish between short- and long-term collaboration. Short-term collaboration is generally geared to on-demand problem solving and tends to involve activities such as one-off training sessions, consulting, testing, and contract R&D services. Long-term collaboration often includes joint R&D projects and is more strategic and open-ended, providing a multifaceted platform for the university and the company to develop innovation activities together.

In Sri Lanka, as in many other developed and developing countries, the majority of links between universities and companies can best be described as short-term, informal interactions with low direct transfer of knowledge and innovation. As we discovered from the questionnaire survey on U-I collaboration, however, there are increasing examples of R&D partnerships between companies and universities in Sri Lanka that are strategic and long-lasting; this is also reflected in the case studies of university-industry collaboration in appendix A. Indeed, all the different types of collaboration mentioned in table 1.3 can be found in Sri Lanka.

**Table 1.3 Typology of University-Industry Collaboration, from Higher to Lower Intensity**

| | | |
|---|---|---|
| High (relationships) | Research partnerships | Inter-organizational arrangements for pursuing collaborative R&D, including research consortia and joint projects |
| | Research services | Research-related activities commissioned to universities by industrial clients, including contract research, consulting, quality control, testing, certification, and prototype development |
| | Shared infrastructure | Use of university labs and equipment by firms, business incubators, and technology parks located near universities |
| Medium (mobility) | Academic entrepreneurship | Development and commercial exploitation of technologies pursued by academic inventors through a company they (partly) own (spin-off companies) |
| | Human resources training and transfer | Training of industry employees, internship programs, postgraduate training in industry, secondments to industry of university faculty and research staff, industry personnel as adjunct faculty |
| Low (transfer) | Commercialization of intellectual property (IP) | Transfer of university-generated IP (such as patents) to firms (e.g., via licensing) |
| | Scientific publications | Use of codified scientific knowledge within industry |
| | Informal interactions | Formation of social relationships (e.g., through conferences, meetings, social networks) |

*Source:* Guimón 2013.

## References

Etzkowitz, H., and L. Leydesdorff . 1997. *Universities and the Global Knowledge Economy: A Triple Helix of University-Industry-Government Relations.* New York: Continuum.

Guimón, J. 2013. "Promoting University-Industry Collaboration in Developing Countries." Policy Brief, Innovation Policy Platform, OECD and World Bank. http://innovationpolicyplatform.org/sites/default/files/rdf_imported_documents /PromotingUniversityIndustryCollaborationInDevelopingCountries.pdf.

World Bank. 2015. *Sri Lanka—Ending Poverty and Promoting Shared Prosperity: A Systematic Country Diagnostic.* Washington, DC: World Bank.

World Economic Forum. 2014. *The Global Competitiveness Report 2014–2015.* Geneva: WEF.

# CHAPTER 2

# Status of and Trends in University-Industry Collaboration in Sri Lanka

## Introduction

This chapter analyzes university-industry (U-I) collaboration in Sri Lanka based mainly on a survey of companies and university departments carried out in 2015. Two structured questionnaires were developed, one for academia and one for industry. The questionnaires were hosted on the website of the Higher Education for the Twenty-First Century Project, and e-mails were sent out to potential respondents, inviting them to participate. Details about the survey methodology and the questionnaires are available in appendix B.

The questionnaires to university academics and industry senior management included questions relating to the areas presented in table 2.1. A similar survey questionnaire was carried out in 2007 with university departments and companies by Dr. Mohamed Esham, who is one of the authors of the present report (Esham 2008). By comparing the two sets of results, it is possible to compare the U-I collaboration activities in 2007 with those reported in 2015.

## University Perspective

This section presents responses from the surveyed universities. It covers the profile of the respondent departments/units/centers, types of U-I collaboration, constraints on U-I collaboration, and suggestions by academics for ways to improve U-I collaboration.

### Profile of the Study Sample

The 2015 study covered all 15 national universities (table 2.2). In total, responses were received from 165 departments, units, and centers in these universities. Seven major disciplines were represented: agriculture, arts, engineering, health sciences, information technology (IT), management, and science.

As shown in tables 2.3 and 2.4, the majority of the respondents were from science-based disciplines. They were mainly department heads and senior lecturers in their respective departments, units, and centers.

**Table 2.1  Main Content of the Questionnaires**

| University questionnaire | Industry questionnaire |
|---|---|
| Department/unit/center information and details of respondents | Company information and details of respondents |
| Services offered to industry | |
| Types of collaboration with industry | Types of collaboration with universities |
| Industrial sectors with which collaborations were undertaken | Benefits of collaboration with universities |
| Coordination of collaborations | Research and development activities |
| Constraints on U-I collaboration | Constraints on U-I collaboration |
| Suggestions for improving U-I collaboration | Suggestions for improving U-I collaboration |

**Table 2.2  Distribution of Academic Respondents, by University, 2015**

| University | Frequency | Percentage |
|---|---|---|
| Eastern University, Sri Lanka | 14 | 8.5 |
| Open University of Sri Lanka | 11 | 6.7 |
| Rajarata University | 11 | 6.7 |
| Sabaragamuwa University of Sri Lanka | 8 | 4.8 |
| South Eastern University of Sri Lanka | 5 | 3.0 |
| University of Colombo | 11 | 6.7 |
| University of Jaffna | 19 | 11.5 |
| University of Kelaniya | 15 | 9.1 |
| University of Moratuwa | 13 | 7.9 |
| University of Peradeniya | 17 | 10.3 |
| University of Ruhuna | 10 | 6.1 |
| University of Sri Jayewardenepura | 16 | 9.7 |
| University of the Visual & Performing Arts | 1 | 0.6 |
| Uva Wellassa University | 4 | 2.4 |
| Wayamba University of Sri Lanka | 10 | 6.1 |
| Total | 165 | 100.0 |

*Source:* Study on Current Status of University-Industry Collaboration in Sri Lanka, 2015.

**Table 2.3  Distribution of Academic Respondents, by Discipline, 2015**

| Discipline | Frequency | Percentage |
|---|---|---|
| Agriculture | 29 | 17.6 |
| Arts | 31 | 18.8 |
| Engineering | 18 | 10.9 |
| Health science | 13 | 7.9 |
| Information technology | 3 | 1.8 |
| Management | 27 | 16.4 |
| Science | 44 | 26.7 |
| Total | 165 | 100.0 |

*Source:* Study on Current Status of University-Industry Collaboration in Sri Lanka, 2015.

Across the university system, as shown in table 2.5, a majority of academics are senior lecturers. On average, each department/unit/center has about two professors, eight senior lecturers, and five lecturers. The average staff strength has improved slightly since 2007.

As far as funding for university departments/units/centers is concerned, almost 50 percent of the responding entities reported having received funds from external sources (table 2.6). However, this figure is lower than the 65 percent that reported external funding in 2007. Funding from international agencies, in particular, has declined, making industry the leading source of external funding in 2015.

Also relevant is the capacity of departments to undertake research and development work in collaboration with industry (figure 2.1). More than 70 percent of surveyed academics state that the facilities available in their departments— particularly laboratory facilities—are inadequate for research, a figure that rose significantly from 50 percent in 2007. The situation thus seems to have deteriorated, even though many universities have purchased equipment utilizing funds made available through two World Bank–funded projects, Improving Relevance and Quality of Undergraduate Education (IRQUE) and the HETC Project. This may be due in part to lack of financial resources to repair and maintain

**Table 2.4  Distribution of Academic Respondents, by Position, 2015**

| Position | Frequency | Percentage |
|---|---|---|
| Dean | 6 | 3.6 |
| Director of unit/center | 1 | 0.6 |
| Head of department | 101 | 61.2 |
| Lecturer | 7 | 4.2 |
| Professor | 10 | 6.1 |
| Senior lecturer | 36 | 21.8 |
| Not specified | 4 | 2.4 |
| Total | 165 | 100.0 |

*Source:* Study on Current Status of University-Industry Collaboration in Sri Lanka, 2015.

**Table 2.5  Composition of Academic Staff in the University System, 2015 and 2007**

| Department/unit/center staff | Number of staff | Average per department/unit/center |
|---|---|---|
| Professor | 304 | 1.8 (1.6) |
| Senior lecturer | 1,248 | 7.6 (6.5) |
| Lecturer | 755 | 4.6 (3.9) |
| Technical staff | 413 | 2.5 (2.4) |
| Administrative staff | 133 | 0.8 (1.4) |

*Sources:* Study on Current Status of University-Industry Collaboration in Sri Lanka, 2015; Study on University Industry (U-I) Interactions in Sri Lanka, 2007.
*Note:* Averages in parentheses are for 2007.

**Table 2.6  External Funding Sources for University Departments, Units, and Centers, 2015 and 2007**

*percentage (frequency)*

| External funding source | 2015a | 2015b | 2007 |
|---|---|---|---|
| Received funds from external sources | 49.7 (82) | 62.9 (56) | 65.2 (30) |
| Industry (private) | 57.3 (47) | 48.2 (27) | 40 (12) |
| Industry (public) | 35.4 (29) | 46.2 (26) | 27 (8) |
| Private foundations | 12.2 (10) | 10.7 (6) | 3 (1) |
| International agencies | 48.7 (40) | 51.8 (29) | 63 (19) |
| Nongovernmental organizations | 8.5 (7) | 5.4 (3) | 17 (5) |
| Did not receive funds from external sources | 50.3 (83) | 37.1 (33) | 34.8 (16) |

*Sources:* Study on Current Status of University-Industry Collaboration in Sri Lanka, 2015; Study on University Industry (U-I) Interactions in Sri Lanka, 2007.
*Note:* 2015a = all 2015 data; 2015b = 2015 data from university departments in disciplines corresponding to the 2007 survey.

**Figure 2.1  Adequacy of University Laboratory Facilities for Teaching and Research, 2015 and 2007**

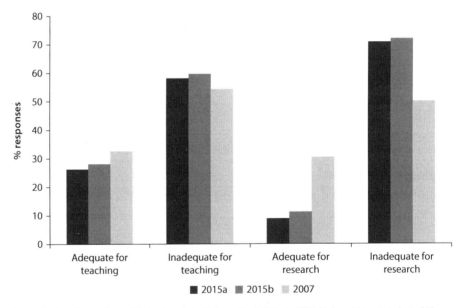

*Sources:* Study on Current Status of University-Industry Collaboration in Sri Lanka, 2015; Study on University Industry (U-I) Interactions in Sri Lanka, 2007.
*Note:* 2015a = all 2015 data; 2015b = 2015 data from university departments in disciplines corresponding to the 2007 survey.

laboratory equipment. In addition, given the rapid pace of technological change since 2007, updating laboratory facilities to meet international standards—and equal the facilities to which many younger faculty have had access in other countries—is expensive and often beyond the reach of Sri Lankan universities. This situation could impede the capacity of universities to collaborate in research and development activities with industry. Also, a large majority of university departments report that they do not have adequate facilities for teaching.

### Types of University Collaboration with Industry

The 2015 survey reveals that 72 percent of the departments are collaborating with industry in some manner, a slight decline from the 2007 figure of 76 percent. The most common type of collaboration is industrial placements of students, followed by research, consultancy, and resource and knowledge sharing (table 2.7). In addition, 11 percent of the engineering departments and 5 percent of the science departments have supported spin-off companies. As expected, engineering and science departments are involved in more U-I collaborations than departments in the humanities and social sciences.

The predominant types of services offered by universities to industry include contract/joint research, consultancy, and seminars (table 2.8). Overall research undertaken on behalf of industry increased significantly in 2015 compared to 2007. The figure for contract research declined only because the research category was split into contract and joint research in 2015. When one considers only 2015 data from university departments in disciplines corresponding to the 2007 survey, slight improvements can be seen in the use of patents and prototypes developed by universities (see figure 2.2). There is also a significantly lower offering of training for company employees in 2015 than in 2007 (table 2.9).

When services are analyzed based on the seven major disciplines (table 2.8), it is clear that engineering and IT-related departments are offering the most services to industry, followed by agriculture, science, and management departments. Humanities departments have offered fewer services to industry but have significantly increased their collaboration in, for example, R&D. Overall, however, there is no major difference in the disciplinary pattern between the two periods.

The coordination of university-industry collaborations has been undertaken mainly by individual academics and the deans/department heads (table 2.10). In addition, there has been progress since 2007 in the involvement of research teams in coordinating collaborations. This indicates a shift from individual research to team-based research for industry, possibly due to the increase in demand for multidisciplinary research. U-I interaction cells are also engaged in coordination. These cells were set up as to act a one-stop shop at each university with a mandate to strengthen collaboration between the university and

**Table 2.7  Types of University Collaboration with Industry, 2015**
*percentage (frequency)*

| Collaboration | Agriculture | Arts | Engineering | Health science | IT | Management | Science | Total | Percentage |
|---|---|---|---|---|---|---|---|---|---|
| Research | 66 (19) | 23 (7) | 67 (12) | 31 (4) | 100 (3) | 26 (7) | 46 (20) | 72 | 44 |
| Consultancy | 41 (12) | 23 (7) | 83 (15) | 23 (3) | 100 (3) | 33 (9) | 34 (15) | 64 | 39 |
| Industrial placements | 66 (19) | 16 (5) | 78 (14) | 0 (0) | 67 (2) | 78 (21) | 55 (24) | 85 | 52 |
| Resource and knowledge sharing | 45 (13) | 32 (10) | 44 (8) | 15 (2) | 100 (3) | 56 (15) | 36 (16) | 67 | 41 |
| Patents/licensing | 3 (1) | 0 (0) | 6 (1) | 0 (0) | 0 (0) | 0 (0) | 5 (2) | 4 | 2 |
| Spin-offs | 0 (0) | 0 (0) | 11 (2) | 0 (0) | 0 (0) | 0 (0) | 5 (2) | 4 | 2 |

*Source:* Study on Current Status of University-Industry Collaboration in Sri Lanka, 2015.

Promoting University-Industry Collaboration in Sri Lanka • http://dx.doi.org/10.1596/978-1-4648-0922-4

**Table 2.8  University Services Offered to Industry, by Discipline, 2015**

*percentage (frequency)*

| Service | Agriculture | Arts | Engineering | Health science | IT | Management | Science | Total | Percentage |
|---|---|---|---|---|---|---|---|---|---|
| Consultancy | 41 (12) | 19 (6) | 78 (14) | 31 (4) | 100 (3) | 44 (12) | 41 (18) | 69 | 42 |
| Contract research | 28 (8) | 29 (9) | 33 (6) | 15 (2) | 67 (2) | 19 (5) | 16 (7) | 39 | 24 |
| Joint research | 48 (14) | 16 (5) | 56 (10) | 15 (2) | 67 (2) | 19 (5) | 41 (18) | 56 | 34 |
| Training company employees | 24 (7) | 13 (4) | 33 (6) | 15 (2) | 33 (1) | 48 (13) | 14 (6) | 39 | 24 |
| Postgraduate training | 17 (5) | 13 (4) | 39 (7) | 8 (1) | 33 (1) | 22 (6) | 11 (5) | 29 | 18 |
| Seminars | 45 (13) | 19 (6) | 39 (7) | 23 (3) | 67 (2) | 56 (15) | 30 (13) | 59 | 36 |
| Laboratory facilities | 28 (8) | 0 (0) | 28 (5) | 8 (1) | 0 (0) | 0 (0) | 27 (12) | 26 | 16 |
| University patents | 10 (3) | 0 (0) | 0 (0) | 0 (0) | 0 (0) | 4 (1) | 5 (2) | 6 | 4 |
| Prototypes developed by the university | 14 (4) | 0 (0) | 33 (6) | 0 (0) | 33 (1) | 0 (0) | 5 (2) | 13 | 8 |

*Source:* Study on Current Status of University-Industry Collaboration in Sri Lanka, 2015.

**Figure 2.2  Comparison of University Services Offered to Industry, 2015 and 2007**

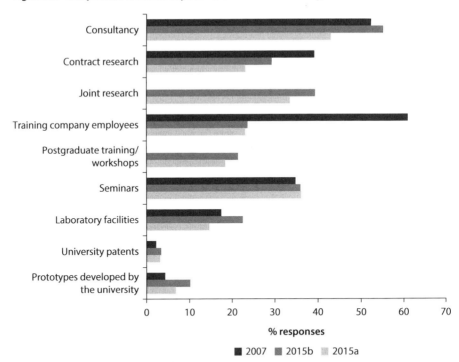

*Sources:* Study on Current Status of University-Industry Collaboration in Sri Lanka, 2015; Study on University Industry (U-I) Interactions in Sri Lanka, 2007.
*Note:* 2015a = all 2015 data; 2015b = 2015 data from university departments in disciplines corresponding to the 2007 survey. Figures are averages across the seven disciplines.

**Table 2.9  University Services Offered to Industry, by Discipline, 2015 and 2007**
*percentage*

| Service | Total | | Engineering | | IT | | Science | | Management | | Humanities | |
|---|---|---|---|---|---|---|---|---|---|---|---|---|
| | 2015 | 2007 | 2015 | 2007 | 2015 | 2007 | 2015 | 2007 | 2015 | 2007 | 2015 | 2007 |
| Consultancy | 55.1 | 52.2 | 94.1 | 91.7 | 100.0 | 20.0 | 46.8 | 56.3 | 71.4 | 25.0 | 25.0 | 22.2 |
| Contract research | 29.2 | 39.1 | 41.2 | 66.7 | 50.0 | — | 19.1 | 43.8 | 42.9 | 25.0 | 37.5 | 22.2 |
| Joint research | 39.3 | — | 58.8 | — | 50.0 | — | 42.6 | | 14.3 | — | 18.8 | |
| Training programs | 23.6 | 60.9 | 35.3 | 75.0 | | 60.0 | 17.0 | 68.8 | 42.9 | 50.0 | 25.0 | 33.3 |
| Postgraduate training | 21.3 | — | 41.2 | — | 50.0 | — | 14.9 | — | — | — | 18.8 | — |
| Workshops | — | 36.9 | | 41.7 | — | 40.0 | — | 43.8 | — | 25.0 | | 22.2 |
| Seminars | 36.0 | 34.8 | 35.3 | 41.7 | 50.0 | 20.0 | 36.2 | 43.8 | — | 25.0 | 31.3 | 22.2 |
| Laboratory facilities | 22.5 | 17.4 | 23.5 | 33.3 | | — | 34.0 | 25.0 | — | — | — | — |
| University patents | 3.4 | 2.2 | — | 8.3 | | — | 6.4 | — | — | — | — | — |
| Prototypes developed by the university | 10.1 | 4.3 | 29.4 | 16.7 | | — | 8.5 | — | — | — | — | — |
| Others | — | 17.4 | — | — | — | 20.0 | — | 25.0 | — | 50.0 | — | 11.1 |

*Sources:* Study on Current Status of University-Industry Collaboration in Sri Lanka, 2015; Study on University Industry (U-I) Interactions in Sri Lanka, 2007.
*Note:* All 2015 data in this table come from university departments in disciplines corresponding to the 2007 survey. — = not available.

**Table 2.10  Coordination of University-Industry Collaborations, 2015 and 2007**
*percentage*

| Coordination | 2015a | 2015b | 2007 |
|---|---|---|---|
| Individual faculty member | 39.4 | 57.3 | 56.5 |
| U-I interaction cell | 10.9 | 14.6 | 10.9 |
| Research team | 15.8 | 22.5 | 6.5 |
| Dean/department head | 35.2 | 27.0 | 34.8 |

*Sources:* Study on Current Status of University-Industry Collaboration in Sri Lanka, 2015; Study on University Industry (U-I) Interactions in Sri Lanka, 2007.
*Note:* 2015a = all 2015 data; 2015b = 2015 data from university departments in disciplines corresponding to the 2007 survey.

industry, resulting in a mutually beneficial partnerships. But their role remains weak, as they are coordinating just 11 percent of current U-I collaborations.

### Academic Perceptions of Constraints to U-I Collaboration

One of the aims of this study was to identify the constraints that university academics may face in their attempts to interact with industry. Participants were asked to evaluate 18 statements on a five-point Likert scale, ranging from 1 (*to a very great extent*) to 5 (*not at all*).

The perceived constraints that inhibit university-industry collaboration at the academic staff level are presented in table 2.11. The dominant responses include lack of time to undertake industry-related research due to heavy academic workload, inadequate laboratory facilities and infrastructure, and lack of proper procedures and mechanisms to facilitate collaboration with industry. These constraints are viewed as more serious in 2015 than they were in 2007. Lack of clear rules on intellectual property rights (IPR) as they apply to university-industry collaboration is also seen as an impediment.

**Table 2.11  Academic Perceptions of Constraints on University-Industry Collaboration, 2015 and 2007**

|  | Mean score | | |
|---|---|---|---|
|  | 2015a | 2015b | 2007 |
| Our research capabilities are not relevant to industry | 3.7 | 3.8 | 3.8 |
| Academics do not feel confident enough to undertake industry-oriented research | 3.8 | 4.0 | 3.9 |
| Lack of motivation among faculty | 3.2 | 3.4 | — |
| Lack of entrepreneurial spirit among faculty | 3.1 | 3.1 | 3.5 |
| Time constraint due to heavy teaching and administrative workload | 1.9 | 1.9 | 2.5 |
| It is not the mission of the academic researcher to collaborate with industry | 4.1 | 4.0 | 4.3 |
| Academics are not aware of the possible channels for getting research sponsorship and consultancy assignments | 2.9 | 3.0 | 3.1 |
| Collaboration with industry has a negative influence on the pedagogic mission of a university | 4.1 | 4.1 | 4.2 |
| Industry is not interested in collaboration with universities | 3.5 | 3.5 | 3.5 |
| Collaboration with industry limits the free choice of research topics | 3.4 | 3.4 | 3.6 |
| Inadequate infrastructure (communication, transport, journals, books) | 2.3 | 2.3 | 3.2 |
| Inadequate laboratory facilities | 2.1 | 2.0 | 3.0 |
| Lack of autonomy to work with industry | 2.9 | 3.0 | 3.4 |
| The university structure is not adapted to the needs of industrial collaborations | 2.8 | 2.7 | 2.9 |
| University norms and procedures hamper collaboration with industry | 2.9 | 2.7 | 2.9 |
| The university has no policy toward collaborations with industry | 2.9 | 2.9 | 3.3 |
| Geographic location of the university results in less access to industry | 3.0 | 3.4 | 3.1 |
| Lack of clear IPR rules for U-I collaboration | 3.0 | 3.1 | — |

*Sources:* Study on Current Status of University-Industry Collaboration in Sri Lanka, 2015; Study on University Industry (U-I) Interactions in Sri Lanka, 2007.
*Note:* Mean scores are based on a Likert scale: 1 = to a very great extent, 2 = to a great extent, 3 = somewhat, 4 = very little, 5 = not at all. Column heads: 2015a = all 2015 data; 2015b = 2015 data from university departments in disciplines corresponding to the 2007 survey. IPR = intellectual property rights. — = not available.

### Academic Perceptions of Measures to Promote U-I Collaboration

Academic participants also expressed their views on the effectiveness of measures to improve university-industry collaboration. Table 2.12 presents these responses on a four-point Likert scale, ranging from 1 (*not at all effective*) to 4 (*very effective*).

The most effective means to promote collaboration, as perceived by academics, are improvement of laboratory facilities, encouragement of industrial visits by academics and students, publicizing university activities relevant to industry, and setting up university-industry interaction cells in the universities. The need to formulate clear rules to allow universities to generate and retain revenues from U-I collaboration is also seen as an important step. There is no significant difference between results from the two periods.

The open-ended question on ways to improve U-I collaboration elicited suggestions to develop curriculum with involvement of industry partners to better

**Table 2.12 Academic Perceptions of Promotional Measures, 2015 and 2007**

| | Mean score | | |
| --- | --- | --- | --- |
| | 2015a | 2015b | 2007 |
| Include industrial internship in the curricula | 3.4 | 3.5 | — |
| Encourage industrial visits by students | 3.5 | 3.5 | 3.5 |
| Encourage regular industrial visits by faculty | 3.5 | 3.5 | 3.5 |
| Improve laboratory facilities | 3.7 | 3.8 | 3.6 |
| Involve staff from industry in teaching programs | 3.3 | 3.2 | 3.2 |
| Set up U-I interaction cells in universities | 3.4 | 3.5 | 3.3 |
| Publicize university activities relevant to industry | 3.5 | 3.6 | 3.5 |
| Conduct seminars and workshops for staff from industry | 3.3 | 3.2 | 3.2 |
| Provide tax concessions for companies collaborating with universities | 3.2 | 3.3 | 3.0 |
| Require academics to undertake a certain amount of work with industry | 2.8 | 2.6 | 2.6 |
| Use industry collaboration as a criterion for salary increments and promotions of academics | 2.4 | 2.3 | 2.9 |
| Give academics more autonomy to work with industry | 3.3 | 3.3 | 3.1 |
| Make available public seed money to foster U-I collaboration on R&D | 3.2 | 3.3 | — |
| Formulate clear rules allowing universities to generate and retain revenues from U-I collaboration | 3.3 | 3.3 | — |

*Sources:* Study on Current Status of University-Industry Collaboration in Sri Lanka, 2015; Study on University Industry (U-I) Interactions in Sri Lanka, 2007.
*Note:* Mean scores are based on a Likert scale: 1= not at all effective, 2 = slightly effective, 3 = effective, 4 = very effective. Column heads: 2015a = all 2015 data; 2015b = 2015 data from university departments in disciplines corresponding to the 2007 survey. — = not available.

suit industry needs; conduct applied research; set up forums to build trust between academic and industry partners and take steps to promote attitudinal change among academics; develop an information database for industry; and place academics in industrial settings. Respondents with successful U-I collaborations highlighted success factors such as personal rapport, industrial placement of students, research by multidisciplinary teams, the quality of the graduates produced, proper planning of collaborative activities, and competencies of academics.

## Industry Perspective

This section presents the perspectives of the industry respondents on university-industry collaboration. It first describes the characteristics of the companies that responded to the survey and discusses types of collaboration between industry and universities. This is followed by industry perceptions of constraints on collaboration. Finally, industry suggestions for ways to improve U-I collaboration are presented.

### Profile of the Study Sample

The characteristics of the sample companies are shown in table 2.13. The 2015 sample consisted of 80 companies, of which just over half were private limited liability companies. The sample covered the manufacturing, trading, services, construction, and IT sectors, with the largest share of sampled firms involved in manufacturing. The majority of companies had more than 100 employees and annual turnover of more than SL Rs. 500 million.

### Types of Industry Collaboration with Universities

Companies seeking to resolve technical issues, develop new products, or implement innovations often interact with external sources such as universities to access knowledge, information, and technology to complement their internal R&D capability. The survey attempted to identify such collaborations (figure 2.3). Almost all the companies (95 percent) had at least one type of collaboration under way in 2015. The predominant types of collaborations were university student internships, informal contact with academics, and attendance at seminars,

**Table 2.13  Profile of Respondent Companies, 2015**

*percentage (frequency)*

| | |
|---|---|
| *Status of firm* | |
| Public listed | 26.3 (21) |
| Private limited liability | 53.8 (43) |
| State-owned | 8.8 (7) |
| Other[a] | 11.3 (9) |
| *Sector* | |
| Manufacturing | 42.5 (34) |
| Trading | 2.5 (2) |
| Service | 37.5 (30) |
| Construction | 2.5 (2) |
| Information technology | 11.3 (9) |
| Other | 3.8 (3) |
| *Employment* | |
| Fewer than 100 employees | 23.5 (20) |
| 100–1,000 employees | 32.9 (28) |
| 1,001–2,000 employees | 12.9 (11) |
| More than 2,000 employees | 17.6 (15) |
| *Turnover (SL Rs)* | |
| <20 million | 16.3 (13) |
| <50 million | 6.3 (5) |
| <100 million | 3.8 (3) |
| <500 million | 11.3 (9) |
| >500 million | 51.3 (41) |

*Source:* Study on Current Status of University-Industry Collaboration in Sri Lanka, 2015.
*Note:* Sample is 80 companies; nine companies did not provide turnover data, and six companies did not provide employment data.
a. Partnerships, companies limited by guarantee, and nongovernmental organizations.

symposiums, workshops, and conferences. A comparison with 2007 data reveals improvements in the level of collaboration, particularly as regards involvement of academics in consultancy, contract and joint research, and project assignments. However, an important finding is the low number of more advanced collaborations, such as use of university-held patents, joint research, and formation of spin-off companies. These are likely to contribute significantly to innovation, but they require a more structured approach.

## Situation of Research and Development in Industry

Scholars recognize that R&D activity is an essential ingredient for increasing companies' ability to cope with technological progress. Studies also suggest that investment in R&D is associated with high rates of return (OECD 2007). Annual R&D expenditures by respondent companies are shown in table 2.14.

**Figure 2.3  Types of Collaboration Reported by Industry, 2015 and 2007**

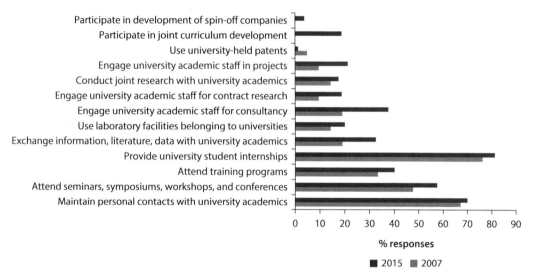

Sources: Study on Current Status of University-Industry Collaboration in Sri Lanka, 2015; Study on University Industry (U-I) Interactions in Sri Lanka, 2007.

**Table 2.14  Annual Research and Development Expenditure as a Percentage of Annual Turnover, 2015 and 2007**

| % of annual turnover | % of companies | |
| --- | --- | --- |
| | 2015 | 2007 |
| <0.5% | 39 | 50 |
| ≥0.5% and <1% | 19 | 22 |
| ≥1% and ≤5% | 23 | 13 |
| >5% | 19 | 16 |

Sources: Study on Current Status of University-Industry Collaboration in Sri Lanka, 2015; Study on University Industry (U-I) Interactions in Sri Lanka, 2007.
Note: 2015 percentages are based on those companies that provided turnover data.

More than one-third of the companies (39 percent) spend less than 0.5 percent of their annual turnover on R&D. This is true even though over half of the sample consists of large companies with annual turnover of more than SL Rs 500 million (table 2.13), and 62 percent of the companies have a separate unit devoted to R&D. However, companies overall did spend a higher percentage of their turnover on R&D in 2015 than in 2007. A large majority of the companies (94 percent) stated that universities should actively engage in R&D activities with outcomes useful for industry.

### Benefits of Collaboration with Universities

To assess the importance of collaboration with universities from the industry point of view, a four-point Likert scale was used to rank the potential benefits, ranging from 1 (*not useful*) to 4 (*highly useful*). Recruitment of high-quality graduates ranks in first position, followed by obtaining access to new ideas and know-how, promoting new product development, and continuous education of staff. Reduction in R&D costs was cited as the least important benefit. There was no significant difference in the rankings between the two periods (table 2.15).

### Industry Perceptions of Constraints on U-I Collaboration

In order to evaluate constraints faced by industry in undertaking collaboration with universities, companies were asked to evaluate 16 constraints on a five-point Likert scale, ranging from 1 (*to a very great extent*) to 5 (*not at all*). The results are presented in table 2.16.

The predominant constraint is the lack of proper mechanisms to facilitate effective collaborations with universities. Other significant obstacles include an apparent lack of entrepreneurial spirit among academics, the low commercialization potential of university research, incompatibility of university structures with the needs of collaboration, and a lack of awareness of facilities and expertise

**Table 2.15  Industry Ranking of Benefits of Collaboration with Universities, 2015 and 2007**

|  | 2015 | | 2007 | |
| --- | --- | --- | --- | --- |
| Benefit | Mean score | Rank | Mean score | Rank |
| Obtain access to new ideas and know-how | 2.90 | 2 | 2.85 | 2 |
| Useful for new product development | 2.81 | 3 | 2.65 | 5 |
| Useful for product improvement | 2.66 | 6 | 2.58 | 7 |
| Useful for quality improvement | 2.67 | 5 | 2.74 | 3 |
| Useful for solving technical problems | 2.59 | 7 | 2.62 | 6 |
| Recruit high-quality graduates | 3.16 | 1 | 3.08 | 1 |
| Reduce in-house R&D cost | 2.58 | 8 | 2.40 | 8 |
| Useful for continuing education of our staff | 2.77 | 4 | 2.67 | 4 |

*Sources:* Study on Current Status of University-Industry Collaboration in Sri Lanka, 2015; Study on University Industry (U-I) Interactions in Sri Lanka, 2007.
*Note:* Mean scores are based on a Likert scale: 1 = not useful, 2 = moderately useful, 3 = useful, 4 = highly useful.

**Table 2.16  Industry Perceptions of Constraints on University-Industry Collaboration, 2015 and 2007**

| | Mean score | |
|---|---|---|
| | 2015 | 2007 |
| Differences between universities and my company in values, mission, or priorities | 3.1 | — |
| Academics are not competent enough to undertake consultancy/ industry-oriented research | 3.3 | 3.3 |
| Lack of motivation among academics | 2.8 | 2.5 |
| Lack of entrepreneurial spirit among academics | 2.5 | 2.5 |
| Low commercialization potential of university research | 2.5 | 2.0 |
| There are no proper mechanisms for collaboration with universities | 2.3 | 1.9 |
| Poor communication between universities and us | 2.6 | 3.6 |
| Most universities lack adequate research facilities | 2.8 | 3.1 |
| Universities are not interested in collaborating with us | 3.0 | 2.3 |
| We are not aware of expertise/facilities available at universities | 2.5 | 2.5 |
| We don't know whom to contact at universities to initiate collaborative activities | 2.7 | 4.1 |
| Our business is not big enough to seek assistance from universities | 4.0 | 3.9 |
| Lack of funds to initiate collaborative work with universities | 3.5 | 2.4 |
| The university structure is not adapted to the needs of industrial collaboration | 2.5 | — |
| Lack of clear IPR rules for U-I collaboration | 2.9 | — |
| The geographic location of our facilities results in less access to universities | 4.0 | 3.9 |

*Sources:* Study on Current Status of University-Industry Collaboration in Sri Lanka, 2015; Study on University Industry (U-I) Interactions in Sri Lanka, 2007.
*Note:* Mean scores are based on a Likert scale: 1 = to a very great extent, 2 = to a great extent, 3 = somewhat, 4 = very little, 5 = not at all. — = not available.

available in universities. A comparison of outcomes from the two periods reveals that communication with university academics and lack of a focal contact point are issues of increasing concern, while availability of funds for initiating collaborations and the interest of universities in collaboration with industry have improved from the industry perspective.

### *Industry Perceptions of Measures to Promote U-I Collaboration*

In order to understand the effectiveness of measures to improve U-I collaboration, industry respondents were asked to evaluate 12 different suggestions on a four-point Likert scale, ranging from 1 (*not at all effective*) to 4 (*very effective*). The results are presented in table 2.17.

Among the promotional measures, student internships, industrial visits by academics and students, involvement of industry resource persons as teaching faculty, and informal gatherings of academic and industry representatives were reported as the most effective measures. Compared to the 2007 survey, industry

**Table 2.17  Industry Perceptions of Promotional Measures, 2015 and 2007**

|  | Mean score | |
|---|---|---|
|  | 2015 | 2007 |
| Include industrial internship in curricula | 3.6 | — |
| Encourage industrial visits by students | 3.6 | 3.3 |
| Encourage regular industrial visits by academics | 3.5 | 3.1 |
| Improve laboratory facilities and other infrastructure at universities | 3.4 | 2.9 |
| Involve staff from industry in teaching programs | 3.6 | 3.2 |
| Publicize university activities relevant to industry | 3.6 | 3.0 |
| Organize joint (university and industry) informal meetings, talks, and communications | 3.6 | 3.1 |
| Government tax concessions for companies collaborating with universities | 3.4 | 2.9 |
| Set up industrial parks closer to universities | 2.9 | 2.6 |
| Encourage academic representation in industry committees/chambers/ boards | 3.4 | 3.0 |
| Encourage industry representation in university committees | 3.4 | 3.1 |
| Make available public seed money to foster U-I R&D collaboration | 3.1 | — |

*Sources:* Study on Current Status of University-Industry Collaboration in Sri Lanka, 2015; Study on University Industry (U-I) Interactions in Sri Lanka, 2007.
*Note:* Mean scores are based on a Likert scale: 1 = not at all effective, 2 = slightly effective, 3 = effective, 4 = very effective. Dashes indicate questions that were not included in the 2007 survey. — = not available.

emphasis on the significance of all the promotional measures has intensified. This may be due to the increased number of U-I collaborations that have taken place since 2007.

The open-ended question on suggestions to improve U-I collaborations elicited the following responses: promote exchange of staff and students and student internships, encourage universities to conduct applied research, promote attitudinal change in both academic and industrial partners, and provide information about the facilities and expertise available in universities. Respondents with successful U-I collaborations highlighted as success factors personal rapport with academics, financial rewards, a memorandum of understanding (MOU) for R&D activities, joint R&D, and producing high-quality graduates.

## Summary of Survey Findings

This chapter has examined the current status of U-I collaborations from the perspective of the two important stakeholders, namely universities and industry. A key conclusion is that both companies and universities are aware of the importance of U-I collaboration and are increasingly willing to finance such collaboration. Overall, the percentage of university departments receiving external funding from any source has not changed significantly from 2007 to 2015 (at least when the same departments are compared), but industry's share of such funding has increased. Private and public industries have emerged as the major external sources of funding for university departments since 2007, while support from international agencies to university departments has declined in terms of its relative share.

The survey findings also show an enhanced emphasis on deeper and more demanding types of collaboration, such as joint R&D activities, prototype testing, and spin-offs, even though these remain relatively uncommon. This has happened in spite of the perception among academics that access to high-quality laboratories and other R&D facilities at their universities has deteriorated. Indeed, a prominent finding is that universities in general are insufficiently equipped to meet the need of companies that would like to collaborate on R&D projects.

Additional conclusions of the surveys, from the university and industry perspectives, may be summed up as follows.

### University Perspective

1. Half of the academic departments in the survey have not been able to attract any external funds and depend on the Treasury for their regular funding.
2. Lack of adequate teaching, laboratory, and infrastructure facilities are cited as a major constraints on opportunities for joint work with industry.
3. The predominant types of university collaboration with industry consist of industrial placements of students, followed by research, consultancy, and sharing of knowledge and resources.
4. U-I collaborations are mainly coordinated and managed by academics or the dean/department head. There has been an increase in the involvement of research teams in managing U-I collaborations since 2007. Generally speaking, the U-I cells set up in universities have not been significantly involved, as they are only coordinating about 11 percent of the existing collaborations.
5. Academics cite heavy workload, inadequate laboratory facilities, and lack of effective mechanisms for collaboration with industry as major constraints. The importance of these factors has not changed significantly since 2007.
6. Upgrading of laboratory facilities, encouragement of staff and student visits to industry, and promotion of university activities relevant to industry are proposed as important measures to promote U-I collaboration. There is also a need to develop clear rules to govern the generation and use of revenues from U-I collaboration, and to make seed money available to foster U-I collaboration in R&D.
7. Academics engaged in successful U-I collaboration attributed their success to factors such as personal rapport with industrial partners, industrial placement of students, multidisciplinary research teams, quality of the graduates produced, proper planning of collaborative activities, and experience and competencies of academics.

### Industry Perspective

1. The predominant types of collaborations are of low and medium intensity, as defined in table 1.2, consisting mainly of university student internships, informal contacts between academic and industry partners, and attendance at seminars, symposiums, workshops, and conferences. However, comparison with 2007 data reveals improvements in the level of collaboration, with academics increasingly involved in consulting, contract and joint research, and project assignments with industry, all of which demand more intense interaction. Humanities and social science departments in particular have significantly increased their collaboration with industry, especially in R&D, albeit from a low level.

2. Companies that responded to the survey are, in general, spending more on R&D as a percentage of company turnover compared to 2007. However, although 62 percent of the companies reported having an in-house unit devoted to R&D, more than 50 percent of the companies invested less than 1 percent of annual turnover in R&D.

3. According to the companies, the most important benefits of U-I collaboration are recruitment of high-quality graduates, obtaining access to new ideas and know-how, and new product development. There is no significant difference in the rankings of the mentioned benefits between the two periods.

4. The predominant constraint appears to be the lack of proper mechanisms for collaboration with universities. Also mentioned were lack of entrepreneurial spirit among academics, the low commercialization potential of university research, unsuitability of university structures for collaboration, and lack of awareness of facilities and expertise available in universities. Comparison of the two periods reveals that communication with the university and lack of a focal contact point are issues of concern, while funds for initiating collaborations and university interest in collaboration have improved.

5. Industry suggestions for improvement of U-I collaboration include steps to promote student internships, industrial visits by academics and students, involvement of industry resource persons as teaching faculty, and informal interactions between academic and industry representatives.

6. Companies suggest that factors such as personal rapport with academics, financial rewards, MOUs for R&D activities, joint R&D, and producing high-quality graduates are vital for successful collaboration.

## References

Esham, M. 2008. "Strategies to Develop University-Industry Linkages in Sri Lanka." Research Studies on Tertiary Education Sector, Study Series 4 (2007/2008), National Education Commission, Colombo.

OECD (Organisation for Economic Co-operation and Development). 2007. *Innovation and Growth: Rationale for an Innovation Strategy*. Paris: OECD.

**CHAPTER 3**

# Policies to Promote University-Industry Collaboration in Sri Lanka and Other Countries

The findings of the 2015 survey suggest that university-industry (U-I) collaborations are often not as easy and straightforward to implement as one would hope. Many companies have found that they do not have proper mechanisms for carrying out joint work with universities. From a business standpoint, educational and research outcomes are not the most important: what matters to a company is how the new knowledge and/or training derived from collaboration with a university can contribute to the company's performance. Does it make possible new products and more effective processes? Are these products and processes patentable, and do they enhance the company's competitive advantage? These are key issues for companies considering partnerships with universities or research institutes (Pertuzé et al. 2010).

For the university, by contrast, the education and research outcomes of collaboration are central as it strives to educate well-prepared graduates and carry out high-quality research. While companies are often interested in turning research and development (R&D) into new patents, products, or processes, and may seek to delay publications to avoid disclosing information, university researchers gain credibility and stature by publishing their results in peer-reviewed journals. For companies, collaboration is about how to monetize the knowledge at hand to promote revenues. For researchers, it's about career progression—what is required to earn promotions or institutional recognition in order to maximize their career development.

As universities and companies often have different incentives to engage in collaboration, many countries have designed and implemented policies that increase the incentives for both universities and companies to collaborate. Government can thus play an important leadership role in fostering U-I collaboration, as both public policies and regulation are needed to establish an enabling framework. This is reflected in the triple helix concept, which includes government as the third partner.

The following sections briefly review key policies that governments, corporations, and universities have developed in Sri Lanka and several other countries to promote U-I collaboration.

## Government Policies

Public policy can significantly influence U-I collaboration through three main policy instruments: (a) direct and indirect funding to universities and companies; (b) regulatory measures that shape the rules governing collaboration between universities and companies (for example, an intellectual property rights [IPR] scheme); and (c) establishment of intermediate organizations such as technology transfer offices (TTOs), science and technology parks, and business incubators.

### Direct and Indirect Funding

Many countries have seen growth in public-private partnerships in science, technology, and innovation that are strategic, long-term, large-scale, high-risk, and multidisciplinary. Such partnerships may involve diverse stakeholders, including government, business, universities, research institutes, and nongovernmental organizations (OECD 2014). They are often initiated by governments through their research and innovation strategies for the purpose of increasing competitiveness and "green" growth.

The most common ways to stimulate university-industry collaboration through direct and indirect funding are by (a) making R&D grants available (including matching grants) on condition that recipients form a consortium of firms and universities to carry out the project, and (b) providing tax incentives for companies that fund collaborative research or buy services from universities. As can be seen in table 3.1, many countries have initiated such direct and indirect public funding to promote U-I collaboration.

R&D grant schemes are often public-private partnerships with private sector co-financing. In Sri Lanka, the country's National Science Foundation is managing a Technology Grant Scheme to promote technology-driven innovations, convert university and research institute R&D outputs into marketable products and services, and encourage the establishment of new technology companies by universities, research institutions, companies, and individuals. The grant scheme also supports joint applications by universities and companies, although joint applications are not a requirement to obtain funding. Additionally, the National Research Council of Sri Lanka has launched the Private-Public Partnership Programme to stimulate R&D activities for economic development.

An example of a joint R&D grant scheme in Malaysia is illustrated in box 3.1. Headquartered in Penang, Collaborative Research in Engineering, Science & Technology (CREST) provides funding to universities and companies for collaborative, market-driven research.

Another example of direct public funding is innovation vouchers, which are small lines of credit provided by governments to small and medium

**Table 3.1  Examples of Direct and Indirect Public Funding to Promote University-Industry Collaboration**

| Policy instrument | Sri Lanka | Other countries |
|---|---|---|
| *Direct public funding* | | |
| **R&D grant schemes** | The National Science Foundation's Technology Grant Scheme is available to universities, public research institutes, and companies individually and as partners. | The Australian Research Council's Linkage Projects Scheme supports R&D collaboration with higher education researchers. |
| | The National Research Council's Private-Public Partnership in R&D Activities for Economic Development involves universities, R&D institutes, corporations, ministries (to provide research expertise), and private or public commercial enterprises. | The European Commission supports collaborative R&D programs. |
| | | The U.S. government's Technology Innovation Program supports research in areas of national need. |
| | | The CREST initiative in Malaysia provides grants for R&D projects. |
| **Innovation vouchers** | | Countries such as Austria, Chile, China, Denmark provide small grants for SMEs to purchase services from universities. |
| *Indirect public funding* | | |
| **Tax incentives** | Tax deductions are given to companies that contract R&D expenditure at a university or research institute. | Tax credits offset companies' payments to universities for the performance of basic research in Italy, Malaysia, and the United States, among others. |

*Note:* CREST = Collaborative Research in Engineering, Science & Technology; SMEs = small and medium enterprises.

---

**Box 3.1  Malaysia's CREST: A Research and Development Matching Grant Program That Supports University-Industry Collaboration**

The Collaborative Research in Engineering, Science & Technology (CREST) program is the first research grant provider that specifically seeks to promote university-industry links in Malaysia's electrical and electronics industry. By providing grants for R&D projects, CREST encourages academic institutions and companies to collaborate on market-driven research. CREST does not operate research labs itself, but funds research located in either universities or industries, as nominated by each research team. Since 2012, CREST has approved 74 projects for matching grants. Both universities and firms participate in every project.

CREST has received a good response from industry by focusing on projects that favor market growth. Through close interactions with industry players, CREST identifies the weak links in strategic segments and sets the direction for the types of R&D to be conducted. In addition, CREST promotes certain cluster programs with the objective of driving local firms to gain higher-value-chain governance at the regional and international levels.

*Source:* Rasiah and Yap 2015.

---

enterprises (SME). The businesses use the credit to purchase services from public knowledge providers who can help them introduce new products, processes, or services in their business operations. From the government's point of view, the main purpose of giving innovation vouchers is to build new relationships between SMEs, universities, and public research institutions that can stimulate knowledge transfer directly and act as a catalyst for the formation of long-term, in-depth relationships (OECD 2010).

In the United Kingdom, the Knowledge Transfer Partnership (KTP) scheme helps businesses innovate and grow by linking them with a university and a recent graduate to work on a specific project. Each KTP is a three-way partnership: the university employs the graduate, who works at the company. A KTP can last from six months to three years, depending on the project and the needs of the business. It is partly funded by a grant from the national government.[1]

In the category of indirect public funding, many countries provide tax incentives to companies that engage in U-I collaboration on R&D. Since 2014, the Sri Lankan government has offered a tax deduction for research and development contracted with a university or research institute. The tax deduction is 300 percent, meaning that the business reduces its taxable income by three times the amount of the contracted R&D expenditure (Mendes 2014: 23).

Governments can also promote U-I collaboration through performance-based funding of universities (table 3.2). The terms of funding may require the university to enter into a minimum numbers of contracts with industry, form a certain number of spin-offs, and so on. The U.K., Canadian, Indian, and Singapore governments, for example, offer universities supplementary funding earmarked for research on condition that they meet such requirements (Yusuf and Nabeshima 2007). Reward systems for researchers have also been launched. In Sri Lanka, university faculty are encouraged to carry out research and can receive a salary bonus of 35 percent if they publish in an internationally or nationally recognized journal, submit a paper to a symposium, or seek a patent and license it.

### Regulating Commercialization of R&D

Much attention is focused on knowledge transfer through publication of university research, the patenting and licensing of academic inventions, and the promotion of

**Table 3.2  Examples of Performance-Based Funding to Promote University-Industry Collaboration**

| Policy instrument | Sri Lanka | Other countries |
|---|---|---|
| **Performance-based funding of universities** | | The United Kingdom, Canada, India, and Singapore offer universities additional funding earmarked for R&D, on condition that the university achieve a certain number of contracts with industry, spin-offs, or start-ups. |
| **Reward systems for researchers** | University faculty can receive a salary bonus of 35 percent if they publish in an internationally or nationally recognized journal, submit a paper to a symposium, or seek and license a patent. | Incentives include research funding from private sources, sabbatical leave to do R&D with private partners, consultancy income, or participation in start-ups. |

university start-ups. The reason for public support for commercialization of public R&D has to do with market and system failures. Weak commercialization of public research may have several causes: (a) potential users may not be aware of university inventions (asymmetric information); (b) industrial partners may be reluctant to engage in commercialization because of unclear risk; (c) demand for research may be weak, as companies, especially SMEs, may not carry out their own R&D; and (d) there may be a lack of funding for developing prototypes and demonstration projects that would help ensure financing for commercialization of university inventions (OECD 2014). Both the U-I collaboration case studies profiled in appendix A and the findings from the survey questionnaires confirm that all these factors come into play in Sri Lanka.

It is considered good international practice to allow public universities and research institutions to take ownership of intellectual property arising from their publicly funded research. Ownership rights are often shared with the individual researcher or research team that produced the invention (Mendes 2014). The researchers are the stakeholders with the greatest immediate motivation to seek commercialization of their invention. In the United States, the Patent and Trademark Law Amendments Act of 1980, also known as the Bayh-Dole Act, governs intellectual property arising from federally funded research. This act permits a university, research institute, small business, or nonprofit institution to pursue ownership of an invention, rather than the government, something that was not permitted before 1980. Many other countries have adopted similar regulation adapted to the circumstances in their country (table 3.3).

In Sri Lanka, there is uncertainty as to whether universities have the legal right to commercialize intellectual property rights. The University Act of 1978, section 29, stipulates that the main mission of universities is teaching and education. The act hardly mentions university research activities, and nothing is included about research commercialization. The 2015 survey on

**Table 3.3  Examples of Intellectual Property Regulation for Universities and Public Research Institutes**

| Policy instrument | Sri Lanka | Other countries |
|---|---|---|
| **Intellectual property rights (IPR policies)** | National IPR regulation does not specify the ownership of inventions based on public R&D carried out at universities and public research institutes. | In the United States, the Bayh-Dole Act permits a university, research institute, small business, or nonprofit institution to pursue ownership of an invention that has been funded by public resources. |
| | The National Science Foundation has adopted international good practice by assigning to grant recipients the ownership of IPR arising from research that it funds. | Other countries, including Brazil, China, South Africa, Malaysia, and the Philippines, as well as several OECD members, have adopted similar regulation adapted to the circumstances in their country (Zuniga 2011). |
| | The University of Moratuwa has developed its own IPR rules. | |

U-I collaboration in Sri Lanka showed that the number of university departments developing patents and prototypes has increased since 2007, and the number of joint and contract research activities has also grown. Both university and industry respondents stated that the lack of clear rules on ownership of IPR from publicly funded R&D is a constraint to U-I collaboration. Another uncertainty facing universities is whether they can set up a company and seek capital for running it. The University of Colombo School of Computing is facing this issue, as mentioned in its U-I collaboration case study in appendix A. Establishing clear IPR and ownership rules for publicly funded research at universities and public research institutes (PRIs) would be an important means to promote joint R&D activities between universities and companies and to develop appropriate technology and innovation capabilities and links in Sri Lanka.

It is also important to understand the micro aspects of U-I collaborations. In Sri Lanka, Public Finance Circular 380 regulates consultancies by universities and research institutes (Department of Public Finance 2000). The guidelines sometimes significantly reduce the ability of researchers to respond in a timely way to industry demands in today's rapidly changing business environments. The rules could be made more flexible to cover the whole range of U-I collaboration activities and to make possible a faster response to industry demands.

Several countries have launched initiatives to facilitate standard licensing agreements between universities and industries. An example is the United Kingdom, which has developed the Lambert toolkit, providing decision guidelines, model agreements, and other materials for negotiations involving universities and companies.[2] Such models for license agreements between universities and industries could also be developed in Sri Lanka.

### Establishing Intermediate Organizations

Governments are creating intermediate organizations or industrial extension agencies to bridge the gap between universities and firms. National governments, regional provinces, and municipalities are also providing land and infrastructure close to universities to attract firms to locate there, often in science and technology parks. Governments are also providing angel and venture capital through quasi-state agencies for university-based start-ups as well as business incubators.

The number of science and technology parks has multiplied in both developed and developing countries. There are, however, numerous examples of failed science and technology parks. In developing countries in particular, quite a few such parks have turned into real estate ventures, often with unsustainable financials. Sri Lanka has not yet sought to develop science and technology parks in the vicinity of universities. However, the Sri Lanka Institute of Nanotechnology (SLINTEC), a public-private research partnership, has established a Nano Science Park. Five companies own 50 percent of SLINTEC, and an additional company has recently joined as well.

Orion City and Trace Expert City IT parks also house several start-ups. It is likely that several of the entrepreneurs in these parks are graduates of Sri Lankan universities.

The Lankan Angel Network (LAN) has recently been established and consists of individual venture capitalists and angel investors. The first of its kind in Sri Lanka, LAN was launched to mobilize the Sri Lankan investor and mentor community to grow the start-up ecosystem. The number of start-ups receiving angel funding has grown fast in recent years, although from a very low starting point. LAN has also financed university start-ups. In addition, the National Science Foundation is managing a scheme to support start-up businesses based on novel technologies, available to researchers in universities and PRIs as well as to individual entrepreneurs.

The U-I collaboration case studies reveal the need to better bridge the funding gap (often referred to as the "valley of death") between basic research and the commercialization of a new product. Many faculty and student inventors at universities find it difficult to access funding, and they also often need technical assistance to develop sustainable business models. The University of Moratuwa (UOM) has decided to invest its own funds in early-stage financing to support the university's home-grown entrepreneurs.

## Corporate Policies

Companies around the world are increasingly are aware of the potential gain in competitiveness from investing in research and innovation (OECD 2007). Much of this investment is performed by larger companies rather than SMEs, as high transaction costs often make it difficult for small firms to engage with universities. An exception is software development start-ups, where the initial capital requirement is often modest.

In particular, multinational companies and large national companies are banking on innovation to sustain and improve their competitiveness, and they have the information, finances, and capacity to manage and benefit from R&D projects with universities. They are also interested in reducing their innovation costs and are tapping into a wide range of disciplines and technologies as well as moving toward open innovation practices. A result of these trends is that open innovation practices coincide with efforts made by universities themselves to increase collaboration with industry and the society at large (Yusuf and Nabeshima 2007).

In Sri Lanka, the business community is likewise aware that collaboration with universities and research institutes is important. At the Sri Lanka Economic Summit 2014, the chairman of the Ceylon Chamber of Commerce made it a point to mention the role of R&D and private sector links in preparing Sri Lanka for a "post-US$4,000 per capita income era." The case studies show that there are examples of fruitful U-I collaborations and that the engagement of academics in consulting, contract and joint research, and project assignments with industry has intensified, albeit from a very low level.

However, the majority of manufacturing and service companies in Sri Lanka are SMEs, which often do not have the capacity to invest in and benefit from innovation and technology development. A study of 140 manufacturing SMEs in the Western Province of Sri Lanka found that they are moderately engaged in product, service, and process innovations, but almost all recorded this process as being new to the firm. Many of the SMEs work in isolation and are inward-oriented, with limited channels for information about technology development and innovation opportunities (Weerasinghe, Jayawardane, and Ramlogan 2013). The study concludes that there is a need to promote innovation at SMEs through closer links and supportive infrastructure with research institutes, universities, and technology support centers.

## University Policies

Although most universities around the world have few formal links with the business sector, the economic, technological, and business environments are evolving to feature more interlinked and open innovation practices. Furthermore, universities in most countries are becoming more autonomous and at the same time more accountable to society for delivering high-quality, relevant education and research. This has spurred a growing competition among universities nationally and internationally to achieve excellence by attracting the best talent. These trends imply that university leadership as well as a larger share of faculty are seeking to collaborate with companies at the regional, national, and international levels. At the same time, local and national governments are offering more incentives to universities and companies to collaborate.

There are many ways in which universities themselves can strengthen their engagement with industry. An increasing number of universities across countries have representatives from industry and civil society on their university and faculty boards. Similarly, a growing number of companies have prominent academics on their corporate boards. This has strengthened a common understanding and awareness of their different cultures and opened the way for stronger interactions and collaboration in education and R&D.

Many top universities around the world have taken steps to institutionalize collaboration with industry. For example, universities increasingly train PhD students and researchers for diverse careers through integration of industry experience into their training and through promotion of industry-relevant PhD projects. They may ask businesses to offer internships and employment to researchers or sponsor research professorships. Denmark's long-standing Industrial PhD Programme places students in private companies, with the time equally divided between industry and university during their research.[3] Malaysia's Industrial Attachment Programme is similar. Such engagement with industry can lead to work-integrated learning opportunities that improve students' work readiness and employability; faculty can also gain exposure to industry environments.

Over the last couple of decades, universities have created "open innovation spaces" and business incubators that provide researchers and students access to good IT infrastructure and an opportunity to work in teams on R&D. Those that have done so include many of the Indian Institutes of Technology and Indian Institutes of Management, along with several of the best universities and colleges in India. They have created hundreds of such open spaces for students and researchers and are also inviting companies to join these spaces (Danish Agency for Science, Technology and Innovation 2016).

Universities in Sri Lanka are also seeking to foster innovation, business incubators, and an entrepreneurial culture within their university communities and with other stakeholders. The formal channels for U-I collaboration through the established U-I interaction cells, however, are not working well in many cases. The coordination of U-I collaboration has been undertaken mainly by individual academics, research teams, and deans/department heads. The role of the U-I interaction cells is generally weak, as they are coordinating less than 11 percent of the collaborations. It seems that the leaders of universities in general have not staffed the U-I interaction cells with employees who have the right level of business experience, and that the units have not been able to engage with businesses in a regular and systematic way.

There are exceptions, however. The case studies of the UOM demonstrate that this university has several years of experience in collaborative research with industry. Recently, the university has created a position at the university for a part-time director of enterprise whose job would be to create new products and processes and promote their commercialization, to establish a business incubation model to strengthen the start-up community in Sri Lanka, to support the development of SMEs through incubation and technology transfer, and to establish a sustainable financing mechanism for start-ups through access to capital from government, the private sector, and international agencies as well as venture capital.

In the United States, many universities have established TTOs. These are responsible for starting the commercialization of university-based innovation and entrepreneurship, supporting licensing and patenting, as well as linking faculty and students with potential investors. Some TTOs are also taking a greater role in organizing networks across university communities, growing their teams in order to better understand new technologies and developing shared university strategies around fundraising, alumni engagement, and corporate relations (U.S. Department of Commerce 2013).

Several universities in Sri Lanka are likewise seeking to deepen their involvement in U-I collaboration by promoting commercialization of new products and processes and establishing business incubators. International experiences have shown that the number one challenge for business incubators is reaching financial sustainability. It often takes time to arrive at the right revenue model and to manage the expectations and demands of a variety of stakeholders while remaining focused on developing the start-up. The second challenge for business incubators is to put in place management teams with the right skills set. Many of them are struggling to get their "selling proposition" and/or pricing right (Khalil and Olafsen 2009: 80). The case study on the Rubber Products and Process Development Incubator at the UOM, for example, mentions that one of its challenges is the lack of a proper marketing arm to market novel products developed by the incubator. It is important that business incubators be set up to operate in a business-minded way and that they forge partnerships with the private sector early in the process of developing a company.

The workshop on Promoting University-Industry Collaborations in Sri Lanka, held in Colombo in 2016, discussed the role of universities in contributing to regional and local development through collaboration with industry, service companies, and local communities. Examining the development benefits of such collaboration more broadly, the Organisation for Economic Co-operation and Development (OECD) reviewed the role of higher education in regional and urban development in 14 regions/cities and 11 countries. It found that stronger interaction and collaboration between higher education institutions and their local and regional communities offers tangible advantages to both sides. Universities often benefit from improved local funding and partnership opportunities for research, teaching, and consultancies; social capital support; and resource-sharing opportunities related to infrastructure and staff. Cities and regions benefit through new businesses generated by faculty and students, enhanced local human capital through graduate retention and continuing education, and generation of tax and other revenues.[4]

The findings of both the U-I collaboration survey and the case studies indicate that IPR regulations and ownership rules in relation to publicly funded research at universities and PRIs are often not clear. The UOM has taken the initiative to develop its own intellectual property policy. This policy states that "UOM shall be the owner of all inventions(s) including software, designs and integrated circuit layouts created by UOM personnel and/or non-UOM personnel, associated with any activity of UOM." It also stipulates that "the earnings less related expenses from the commercialization of IP owned by UOM shall be shared between UOM and the Inventor/Author/Designer at the rate of Inventor(s) share: 60% and UOM's share: 40% and such payments becoming due and payable on receipt of payments from the licensees" (UOM 2010: 10).

Both Colombo and Moratuwa Universities are engaged in expanding their educational curricula and programs in entrepreneurship for undergraduate and graduate students. Entrepreneurship courses and programs aim to equip students with a wide range of skills, including business plan development, fundraising, marketing, networking, and connecting with local business leaders, for example through mentorship arrangements. In India, an institution that is taking a systematic approach to developing students' entrepreneurial skills is the B. V. Bhoomaraddi College of Engineering and Technology in Hubli, which has developed a Centre for Technology Innovation and Entrepreneurship (box 3.2).

**Box 3.2  B. V. Bhoomaraddi College of Engineering and Technology: Fostering an Entrepreneurial Culture in Engineering Education**

The BVB College of Engineering and Technology in Hubli, India, has systematically sought to build a business ecosystem with the following elements: (a) focus on local economic and social needs; (b) engage external entrepreneurs to kick-start the ecosystem; (c) support deserving enterprises to showcase early winners; (d) connect the start-up success to develop a culture of entrepreneurship on campus; (e) nurture and strengthen entrepreneurial culture through curriculum interventions; and (f) go global and benchmark.

The college has set up the Centre for Technology Innovation and Entrepreneurship in order to develop entrepreneurial thinking and encourage students to take on socially relevant challenges. Since its start in 2012, the center has hosted 34 companies and has created 230 jobs in the region. Of the 34 companies, 23 percent were started by students and recent graduates. Several of the start-up companies have received angel and venture capital funding from Indian and foreign investors.

*Source:* Kulkarni, Shettar, and Atre 2016.

## Notes

1. Information on the KTP scheme is available at https://www.gov.uk/guidance/knowledge-transfer-partnerships-what-they-are-and-how-to-apply.

2. Information on the Lambert toolkit is available at https://www.gov.uk/guidance/lambert-toolkit.

3. Information on the Danish Industrial PhD is available at http://innovationsfonden.dk/en/application/erhvervsphd.

4. The OECD's reports on higher education in regional and city development are available on the website of the OECD Higher Education Programme, http://www.oecd.org/edu/imhe/highereducationinregionalandcitydevelopmentreviewreportsandvisits.htm.

## References

Danish Agency for Science, Technology and Innovation. 2016. *Entrepreneurship and Start-Up Activities at Indian Higher Education Institutions.* IDCK Analysis 3. Copenhagen: Ministry of Higher Education and Science.

Department of Public Finance of Sri Lanka. 2000. Public Finance Circular 380. "Guidelines for Undertaking Consultancy Work by Universities and Research & Development (R&D) Centres and Their Staff." Colombo.

Khalil, M. A., and E. Olafsen. 2009. "Enabling Innovative Entrepreneurship through Business Incubation." In *The Innovation for Development Report 2009–2010: Strengthening Innovation for the Prosperity of Nations*, edited by A. López-Claros, 69–84. New York: Palgrave Macmillan.

Kulkarni, N., A. Shettar, and M. Atre. 2016. "Integrating Entrepreneurial Ecosystem into Engineering Education: Driving Regional Economy in Tier-2 Cities." *Journal of Engineering Education Transformations*, Special Issue. doi:10.16920/jeet/2016 /v0i0/85712.

Mendes, P. 2014. *Integrating Intellectual Property into Innovation Policy Formulation in Sri Lanka.* Geneva: World Intellectual Property Organization.

OECD (Organisation for Economic Co-operation and Development). 2007. *Innovation and Growth: Rationale for an Innovation Strategy.* Paris: OECD.

———. 2010. "Innovation Vouchers." OECD Innovation Policy Platform, Paris.

———. 2014. *OECD Science, Technology and Industry Outlook.* Paris: OECD.

Pertuzé, J. A., E. S. Calder, E. M. Greitzer, and W. A. Lucas. 2010. "Best Practices for Industry-University Collaboration." *Sloan Management Review* 51 (4): 83–90.

Rasiah, R., and X. Yap. 2015. "Innovation Performance of the Malaysian Economy." In *The Global Innovation Index 2015: Effective Innovation Policies for Development*, 139–46. Geneva: WIPO; Ithaca, NY: Cornell University; Fontainebleau, France: INSEAD.

UOM (University of Moratuwa). 2010. "Intellectual Property Policy." Katubedda, Moratuwa, Sri Lanka. http://www.mrt.ac.lk/ipac/files/IP%20Policy.pdf.

U.S. Department of Commerce. 2013. *The Innovative and Entrepreneurial University: Higher Education, Innovation and Entrepreneurship in Focus.* Washington, DC: U.S. Department of Commerce.

Weerasinghe, R. N., A. K. W. Jayawardane, and R. Ramlogan. 2013. "Innovation for the Bottom of Economic Pyramid: The Role of Manufacturing SMEs in Sri Lanka." Presented at conference on New Models of Innovation for Development, University of Manchester, U.K, July 4.

Yusuf, S., and K. Nabeshima, eds. 2007. *How Universities Promote Economic Growth.* Washington, DC: World Bank.

Zuniga, P. 2011. "The State of Patenting at Research Institutions in Developing Countries: Policy Approaches and Practices." WIPO Economic Research Working Paper 4, World Intellectual Property Organization, Geneva.

# University-Industry Collaboration in Sri Lanka: Possible Ways Forward

As Sri Lanka seeks to become an upper-middle-income country, it will have to develop and produce more knowledge-intensive products and processes that are globally competitive, just as Singapore, the Republic of Korea, and Taiwan, China, did in recent decades. Strengthening university-industry (U-I) collaboration in Sri Lanka, as part of an effort to improve the country's overall capacity for research and innovation, is an important prerequisite for such progress. The majority of collaborations between companies and universities in Sri Lanka, as in many other countries, are informal and short-term, with low direct transfer of knowledge and innovation. There are, nonetheless, some good examples of formal R&D partnerships between companies and universities that are strategic, long-term, and of mutual benefit to both partners, as demonstrated by the case studies.

This chapter discusses possible ways to strengthen U-I collaboration in Sri Lanka. The suggestions are based on the findings in chapters 1–3, the case studies in appendix A, and discussions at the stakeholder workshop on Promoting University-Industry Collaborations in Sri Lanka (see appendix C).

Participants at the 2016 workshop were given a list of policy proposals based on a preliminary analysis of the 2015 survey. They divided into four working groups focused on the following areas:

- Strengthening overall innovation policy
- Policy reforms for strengthening U-I collaboration
- Strengthening mobility between universities and companies
- Providing better access to information on research and innovation

In these working groups, they discussed and revised the draft proposals and added new ones. Each of the four groups then presented its suggestions to all the participants in a plenary session. Taking into account the recommendations of the workshop participants, the authors developed the final recommendations presented in this chapter. The suggestions are grouped into four sections corresponding to the topics listed above.

## Strengthening the Overall Innovation Policy Framework

Sri Lanka's innovation policy framework is formulated in its Science, Technology & Innovation Strategy 2011–2015. This strategy aims to build, over time, a well-functioning national innovation system with high-quality entrepreneurs and researchers, one that fosters synergies between universities, research institutes, business incubators, and companies. This framework is now being updated for the period 2016–20. The participants at the workshop suggested that the Science, Technology & Innovation Strategy 2016–2020 will create stronger links between universities, research institutes, and companies, with an appropriate intellectual property rights (IPR) regime and a financing system that stimulates early-stage financing of research-intensive start-ups. Building a well-functioning innovation system over several years would make it easier to establish stronger U-I collaboration.

It is also suggested that the national innovation policy will map the research and technology competences of universities and PRIs in different scientific fields, based on the expertise, infrastructure, and facilities of each of them. Peradeniya University may make an ideal hub for agriculture-related research and technologies, for example, while Moratuwa University may be the best place to tackle electronics. Prioritization of scarce resources for research, including human resources and infrastructure, is necessary to build high-quality centers with expertise in the scientific fields that are most important to Sri Lanka's key economic sectors.

Good research infrastructure is a critical part of ensuring high-quality research. However, more than 70 percent of the academics who responded to the U-I collaboration survey in 2015 stated that the R&D facilities available in their departments are inadequate for performing research. This marked a significant increase from 50 percent in 2007. This strongly suggests that Sri Lankan universities in general are not well equipped to meet the needs of companies that would like to collaborate on R&D projects. The participants at the 2016 workshop therefore called for a national mapping of the needs for improvements to research infrastructure at universities and PRIs. The Sri Lanka Institute of Nanotechnology (SLINTEC) is a good example of a collaborative effort between the public sector and private companies to build national-level research capacity in a specific field, in this case nanotechnology.

Table 4.1 provides an overview of suggested initiatives for strengthening overall innovation policy in the short and medium-to-long terms, including organizations that would be responsible for implementing each initiative.

**Table 4.1  Suggested Initiatives to Strengthen the Overall Innovation Policy Framework**

| Initiative | Short term (within 6–12 months) | Medium to long term (within 1–5 years) | Actors |
|---|---|---|---|
| Build a national innovation ecosystem | The Sri Lanka government's Science, Technology & Innovation Policy 2016–2020 is being drafted. It is important that the business sector be involved in this process. | Draft and implement the Science, Technology & Innovation Policy 2016–2020, with a strong focus on prioritization of research funding and efforts to foster stronger links between domestic and foreign firms as well as between universities, R&D institutions, and business sectors. | Ministry of Finance; Ministry of Science, Technology and Research; other relevant ministries; universities and public research institutes (PRIs); companies and business associations. |
| Improve the research infrastructure | Drafting of the Science, Technology & Innovation Policy 2016–2020 should include a national mapping of the needs for improvement to research infrastructure at universities and PRIs. | Develop a national mapping of research infrastructure needs in line with the national research and innovation priorities. Implement the national research infrastructure plan. | Ministry of Science, Technology and Research; Ministry of Higher Education and Highways; University Grants Commission; other relevant ministries. |

## Policy Reforms to Strengthen University-Industry Collaboration

Government policies play a major role in creating a national innovation system in which U-I collaboration can flourish. In Sri Lanka both the National Science Foundation (NSF) and the National Research Council (NRC) are managing programs for joint university and industry research. The participants at the workshop called for efforts to review and strengthen the existing research funding schemes that explicitly fund research collaboration between universities, research institutes, and companies.

Sri Lanka has introduced tax incentives to promote U-I collaboration on R&D. Companies can obtain a tax reduction of 300 percent of the R&D expenditures when they contract research to a university or a research institute. Workshop participants suggested evaluating the implementation efficiency of the tax incentives to ensure that the program really does strengthen I-U collaboration. They also proposed introduction of a pilot program on innovation vouchers.

Both the U-I collaboration survey and the case studies show the need to strengthen intermediate organizations and industrial extension agencies, including access to early-start financing to bridge the gap between universities and firms, especially SMEs. This can be done by supporting angel and venture capital through quasi-state agencies for university-based start-ups. Professional support is also needed from experienced business consultants, who can help entrepreneurs and researchers develop the right management and revenue models as they create their start-ups, for example through business incubators.

It is proposed that universities establish open innovation spaces and business incubators where faculty, students, and company personnel can work together. They should also promote student entrepreneurship through courses, competitions, and awards. Universities should revamp the U-I interaction cells by bringing in staff with professional expertise in technology transfer and business model development. This should be done in collaboration with business development experts and angel and venture capital companies.

There is a need to develop clear IPR and ownership rules for publicly funded research at universities and PRIs, as well as standard license agreements between universities and industries. Instruments such as the Lambert toolkit in the United Kingdom could be customized to the needs of Sri Lanka. Such a tool would facilitate U-I collaboration by providing decision guidelines, model license agreements, and other materials for negotiations between universities and companies.

There is also a need to examine the extent to which the rules prescribed in Public Finance Circular 380 can be made more flexible, so that universities can respond faster to industry demands. It will be difficult for Sri Lanka to scale up U-I collaboration on joint R&D activities and to develop the necessary technology and innovation capabilities and links without also modernizing the financial management rules that govern university engagement in U-I collaboration.

A final suggestion is to disseminate the experiences of successful U-I collaborations by establishing a platform for networking. This could be done through a yearly conference under the auspices of the Ministry of Science, Technology and Research, the Ministry of Universities and Highways, and UGC.

Table 4.2 provides an overview of suggested initiatives for improving U-I collaboration through policy reforms in the short and medium-to-long terms, including organizations that would be responsible for implementing each initiative.

**Table 4.2 Suggested Initiatives for Policy Reforms to Strengthen University-Industry Collaboration**

| Initiative | Short term (within 6–12 months) | Medium to long term (within 1–5 years) | Actors |
|---|---|---|---|
| Strengthen R&D funding schemes for joint projects between universities/PRIs and companies, based on national and international experiences | Review the funds that have been made available for joint R&D projects in terms of amount, utilization, process, outcomes, management, and implementation. Disseminate information on funding opportunities for universities, PRIs, and companies to encourage U-I collaboration. | Based on the assessment, scale up good practices of existing R&D funding schemes. Carry out implementation, monitoring, and evaluation of the suggested R&D funding schemes. | NRC; NSF; Ministry of Science, Technology and Research; Ministry of Higher Education and Highways; UGC |
| Assess the efficiency of tax incentives for companies that contract R&D to universities | Evaluate the usefulness and efficiency of the current tax reduction of 300 percent for contracted R&D expenditure at a university or PRI. | Based on the assessment, determine whether revisions and/or amendments to the existing tax reductions would be beneficial. | Ministry of Finance; Ministry of Industry and Commerce |

*table continues next page*

**Table 4.2  Suggested Initiatives for Policy Reforms to Strengthen University-Industry Collaboration** (continued)

| Initiative | Short term (within 6–12 months) | Medium to long term (within 1–5 years) | Actors |
|---|---|---|---|
| Introduce innovation vouchers for SMEs | As SMEs often do not have the capacity and resources to do joint R&D with universities or PRIs, design a pilot project on innovation vouchers for SMEs. Encourage business associations to support SMEs to invest in research and innovation. | Launch a pilot project on innovation vouchers for SMEs. If the pilot project is promising, launch a full innovation voucher scheme. | Ministry of Industry and Commerce |
| Establish an IPR policy for publicly funded research | Define and implement clear IPR rules for publicly funded research to encourage the use of research results and ensure effective and timely legal protection of IP inspired by the Bayh-Dole Act. Encourage transparency in the processes for determining the terms, conditions, and profit sharing of technology transfer to inspire confidence in the investment value of supporting research and innovation, from knowledge generation to application. | Authorize universities to develop their own IP policies and licensing agreements within a national framework. Provide structured in-house and external professional training to scientists and entrepreneurs to enable them to better understand and analyze the techno-legal and business information contained in IP documents. | Ministry of Industry and Commence; Ministry of Science, Technology and Research; National Intellectual Property Office; UGC; universities |
| Create better possibilities for universities to retain revenues from U-I collaboration | UGC will work with the Ministry of Finance to revise Public Finance Circular 380 so that the rules are more flexible and enable universities to respond faster to industry demands for R&D, consultancy, and education services, as well as giving the university researchers better incentives to embark on U-I collaboration. | The Ministry of Finance will issue a revised Public Finance Circular on R&D, consultancy, and education services by universities and PRIs. Consider a revision of the existing University Act of 1978 to facilitate U-I partnerships, consultancies, and education services. | Ministry of Finance; Ministry of Higher Education and Highways; UGC; universities and PRIs |
| Establish open innovation spaces and business incubators at universities and make available seed money for faculty and students to develop start-ups | Universities will establish open innovation spaces and business incubators where students, faculty, and companies can work together. Make available seed money for faculty and students for prototype development and start-ups for promising projects. | Universities will systematically promote faculty and student innovation and entrepreneurship through courses, competitions, and awards. Universities will mobilize seed money for faculty and students, through donors, sponsorships, | Ministry of Finance; UGC; Ministry of Higher Education and Highways; Ministry of Science, Technology and Research; universities; business associations; angel and venture capital companies |

*table continues next page*

**Table 4.2  Suggested Initiatives for Policy Reforms to Strengthen University-Industry Collaboration** (continued)

| Initiative | Short term (within 6–12 months) | Medium to long term (within 1–5 years) | Actors |
|---|---|---|---|
| | Make professional business advice and training available to university faculty and students. | endowments, and government programs, for prototype development and creation of start-ups. | |
| | | UGC and universities will revamp the U-I interaction cells with professional expertise in technology transfer and business model development. This should be done in collaboration with business development experts, including angel and venture capital companies. | |
| Disseminate successful case studies of U-I collaboration at high-level events | Under the auspices of the Ministry of Science, Technology and Research, the Ministry of Higher Education and Highways, and UGC, organize an annual conference to disseminate successful U-I collaboration and provide a platform for networking. | Widely disseminate the results and good practices from the national-level events. | Ministry of Science, Technology and Research; Ministry of Higher Education and Highways; UGC; COSTI; NSF; NRC; universities and PRIs; companies |

*Note:* COSTI = Coordinating Secretariat for Science, Technology and Innovation; IP = intellectual property; IPR = intellectual property rights; NRC = National Research Council of Sri Lanka; NSF = National Science Foundation of Sri Lanka; SME = small and medium enterprise; UGC = university grants commission; UI = university-industry.

## Increasing Mobility between Universities and Companies

Universities in Sri Lanka have already built good informal links with companies to make internships available, especially for undergraduate students. It is suggested that these internships be organized in a more formalized way. The best master's and PhD students should have the opportunity to work part-time in a company on targeted research projects while remaining enrolled at a university. In designing such formal partnerships between universities and companies, Sri Lanka could look to the Danish Industrial PhD Programme and the Malaysian Industrial Attachment Program. Universities increasingly need to train PhD students and researchers for diverse careers, for example by integrating industry experience into the training of research students, promoting industry-relevant PhD projects, and asking businesses to offer internships and employment to researchers. Sri Lanka might also consider introducing a program similar to the Knowledge Transfer Partnership scheme in the United Kingdom.

Beyond research training, mobility of staff between academia and industry at all levels is needed to increase collaboration. Exchanges between midcareer and

**Table 4.3  Suggested Initiatives to Increase Mobility between Universities and Companies**

| Initiative | Short term (within 6–12 months) | Medium to long term (within 1–5 years) | Actors |
|---|---|---|---|
| Establish opportunities for master's and PhD students to pursue a targeted research project in a company as part of their study | Make necessary changes in the study rules and curriculum to allow master's and PhD students to pursue targeted research projects in a company as part of their study. | Professionalize student internship programs. More structured internship programs would make it possible for the best students to pursue targeted research projects in a company as part of their study. | University Grants Commission (UGC); universities; companies |
| Establish an industrial PhD program | Design an industrial PhD program for universities, customized to the needs of Sri Lanka and inspired by international experience and good practices. | Implement the industrial PhD program. | UGC; universities; companies |
| Facilitate midcareer and senior staff job exchange between universities and companies | Create more opportunities for midcareer and senior staff job exchange (sabbatical leave, industry-funded research chairs) between universities and companies, supported by the senior leadership of the companies and universities. | | Universities; companies |
| Facilitate mutual board memberships | Universities should invite industry members to sit on university and faculty boards, and industry should invite faculty members to sit on company boards. | | UGC; universities; companies |

senior staff facilitate the sharing of knowledge and deepen engagement between sectors. Activities to increase mobility between universities and companies will reinforce understanding and collaboration between the two partners. Universities might also want to invite representatives from industry to join their university or faculty boards to facilitate and strengthen collaboration, and companies could invite faculty members to sit on their corporate boards.

Table 4.3 provides an overview of suggested initiatives to increase mobility between universities and companies in the short and medium-to-long terms, including organizations that would be responsible for implementing each initiative.

## Providing Better Access to Information on Research and Innovation

Universities, PRIs, and research funding agencies should improve the information they disseminate about their research activities. COSTI has developed the Sri Lanka Innovation Dashboard to provide information about the current status of Sri Lanka's science, technology, and innovation activities. Strong leadership at both national and institutional levels will be necessary to ensure that the dashboard contains reliable, useful, and updated information. This can especially benefit SMEs, which often have little knowledge about opportunities for research and innovation in collaboration with universities. The United Kingdom's Gateway to Research can provide inspiration on how to disseminate information on science, technology, and innovation activities to improve the discoverability and accessibility of all publicly funded research.

An information platform should be established to deliver up-to-date information to inventors, researchers, and entrepreneurs on how to commercialize research results. This should include an overview of the different funding resources and business development advice services available to those setting up a company. The Sri Lanka Inventors Commission (SLIC) could possibly undertake this task if its mandate were widened and its capacity increased.

Table 4.4 provides an overview of suggested initiatives to provide better access to information on research and innovation in the short and medium-to-long terms, including organizations that would be responsible for implementing each initiative.

**Table 4.4  Suggested Initiatives for Providing Better Access to Information on Research and Innovation**

| Initiative | Short term (within 6–12 months) | Medium to long term (within 1–5 years) | Actors |
|---|---|---|---|
| Improve the dissemination of information about research and innovation activities at universities and PRIs | Design and pilot a Web-based database with reliable, useful, and updated information about the current status of Sri Lanka's science, technology, and innovation activities. COSTI has started this work through its Sri Lanka Innovation Dashboard. | Based on the pilot, the Web-based database will be launched, made public, and continuously updated. | COSTI; NSF; NRC; UGC; universities and PRIs |
| Strengthen information on how to commercialize research results and inventions and create start-up companies | Establish an information platform to deliver up-to-date information to inventors, researchers, and entrepreneurs on how to commercialize research results, including an overview of the different funding resources and business development advice services available to those setting up a company. | Based on a pilot, the information platform on how to commercialize research results and inventions and create start-up companies will be launched, made public, and continuously updated. | SLIC; COSTI; NSF; NRC; UGC; universities and PRIs |

*Note:* COSTI = Coordinating Secretariat for Science, Technology and Innovation; NRC = National Research Council of Sri Lanka; NSF = National Science Foundation of Sri Lanka; PRI = public research institute; SLIC = Sri Lanka Inventors Commission; UGC = university grants commission.

# Case Studies on University-Industry Collaboration in Sri Lanka

Four case studies were developed by faculty members at the Universities of Peradeniya, Colombo, Wayamba, and Moratuwa, presenting their institutions' experiences with U-I collaboration. The profiles address issues such as the mutual advantages of collaboration, criteria for successful collaboration, funding and operational models, sharing of experiences, constraints faced during implementation, and barriers to sustainability of the collaboration.

## Case Study 1: University of Peradeniya

### *Veterinary Business Center, Faculty of Veterinary Medicine and Animal Science*

The Faculty of Veterinary Medicine and Animal Science at the University of Peradeniya has established a Veterinary Business Center (VBC) to provide consultancy services for industry, product development, laboratory testing, and training on a commercial basis.

### *Why Did Industry Partner with the University?*

The Faculty of Veterinary Medicine & Animal Science (FVMAS) is the sole veterinary higher education institution in Sri Lanka. Its multidisciplinary research, diverse expertise, low cost, accredited research laboratories, and long-standing history of contribution to veterinary and allied industries are key factors for a successful industry-university business partnership.

### *What Value Did the University Add to Industry?*

The FVMAS has made available novel technologies for animal breeding, effective vaccines, biologicals, feed formulations, and a number of laboratory screening tests for foods of animal origin. The cost-effectiveness of our technologies has served industry immensely. The clinical trials and consultancies undertaken by the FVMAS have led to development of concepts, processes, and products, such as irradiated larval vaccines. Our accredited laboratory tests have ensured that Sri Lankan products of animal origin meet the high quality standards required by the export market, thus making an important contribution to the development of veterinary and allied industry and of the country at large.

### What Did the University Gain from Working with Industry?

The FVMAS benefits from the guidance and mentorship of its industry affiliations. Industry-based placement of veterinary undergraduates helps to develop professional skills and strengthen knowledge. Funding opportunities for researchers are increased by providing equipment, chemicals, consumables, and even payments for research assistance and staff while providing a regular needs assessment for the teaching, learning, and service functions of the FVMAS.

### What Does It Take to Keep this University-Industry Partnership Successful?

Most of the veterinary and allied industries in Sri Lanka are led by our alumni. Ensuring their active participation and involvement in collaborative research, effective engagement, and regular needs assessments of industries is critical to keep this university-industry partnership successful.

### What Can Other Universities Learn from this Case Study?

Other institutes can learn how to capitalize on the strategic advantage of being the only university entity producing professionals for industry. Our experience also shows how alumni can be used for initiation of successful, mutually beneficial partnerships.

### Overview of the Collaboration

As one of the leading service providers in the University of Peradeniya, the FVMAS has earned a high reputation for excellence in services it has rendered to industry and the public over a long period of time. In addition, the faculty provides numerous consultancy services to industry throughout the year. Our state-of-the-art hospitals, accredited research and service laboratories, and well-equipped production and service units, together with dedicated academic, research, and support staff, have underpinned a number of industry-university collaborations. Most have been initiated through the personal contacts of either faculty researchers or our alumni working in industry, and this has led to the development of research outcomes/products with potential for commercialization. Yet commercialization of faculty research outcomes was not considered a priority until recently, primarily due to unavailability of a dedicated entity within the FVMAS organizational framework. The need was first revealed by a self-evaluation report done for the preparation of the FVMAS corporate plan 2010–2015, and in this plan the FVMAS identified establishment of such a dedicated entity for this purpose.

   With financial support from Window 4 of the Higher Education for the Twenty First Century (HETC) Project, funded by the World Bank, the FVMAS has initiated establishment of a dedicated entity for proper dissemination and commercialization of its research outcomes. This entity, the Veterinary Business Center (VBC), will enable better coordination of consultancies undertaken by the FVMAS faculty and encourage innovation among its research staff. The FVMAS Faculty Board has given provisional approval for the VBC but has requested University Council approval for the proposed operational mode. A comprehensive proposal will be submitted to the University Council soon.

Along with the establishment of the VBC, three research outcomes with potential for commercialization were selected for further improvement and development, utilizing the funds from the HETC Project as seed money. The respective laboratories were upgraded with necessary equipment and refurbished to support production. The three research outcomes are as follows:

- *Production of high-quality cattle/goat embryos for the livestock industry:* The advanced reproductive biotechnology laboratory of the FVMAS has success- fully established technologies for production of high-quality cattle and goat embryos for the livestock industry in Sri Lanka. The main partner for this project is the National Livestock Development Board (NLDB), and field trials have proven the success of mass production of high-yielding dairy cattle at low cost. The same technology is currently being used for conservation of indige- nous animal genetic resources, especially the Jaffna breed of sheep, with the partnership of the Department of Animal Production and Health (DAPH). Donor animals are maintained at the veterinary teaching farm, Udaperadeniya. At present, both industry partners are from the government. However, several private farms have initiated work with us on embryo transfer.

- *Production of low-cost and effective irradiated larval vaccines to control gastroin- testinal nematodiasis in ruminants:* An irradiated larval vaccine was devel- oped against the highly pathogenic nematode parasite of goats, *Haemonchus contortus*, with the collaboration of the DAPH and NLDB. The vaccine is cost-effective and easy to use, making it safe to be handled by farmers. The product registration process has already been initiated, and it is expected that goat production will increase with the proper use of this vaccine island- wide. The same laboratory has now developed the capability to produce customized, farm-specific multispecies vaccines upon request. The larval factories are maintained at the FVMAS field research station at Udaperadeniya.

- *Antibiotic residue screening tests and food microbial assays for foods of animal origin:* A number of antibiotic residue screening tests using the HPLC and ELISA technologies have been developed and validated by the Food Safety and Quality Assurance Laboratory (FSQAL) of the FVMAS. They will be made available to industry through the VBC. The FSQAL, an accredited lab- oratory, has several industrial partners representing leading shrimp and poul- try product exporters in the private sector. High-quality screening tests have helped the exporters succeed in highly competitive international markets, and FSQAL is extending the spectrum of new commodities for the tests.

The VBC has its own fully furnished office and support staff (a secretary). Office space is air-conditioned and equipped with desktop computers, laser printers, telephone, fax, and photocopying equipment. A consultant was hired to develop a business and marketing plan for the newly established business center. The VBC has a part-time director and a Management Committee appointed by the FVMAS Faculty Board. Currently, the Management Committee consists of the dean of the faculty, heads of departments, and the activity coordinators of the HETC Project–funded entity (the VBC). According to the business plan developed, it was proposed to have at least two industry partners on the Director Board.

The VBC undertakes projects such as consultancies, product development (vaccines, biologicals, drugs, feed, etc.), laboratory testing, training, and value-adding activities through industrial partnerships. At present, the VBC is owned by the FVMAS and is operated as a unit of the FVMAS under the administrative and financial regulation of the University of Peradeniya. Currently the accounts for the three products concerned are maintained at the respective laboratories. When University Council approval is granted, they will be merged with the VBC account and the VBC accounting system will be fully functional. The VBC maintains accounts separately, and an annual audited account of the VBC is to be regularly presented along with the annual report. Project budgets are prepared before signing of the business partnership agreements; 5 percent of the budget will be given to the FVMAS, and another 5 percent will be allocated to the general fund of the VBC. The remaining 90 percent will cover staff payments, production costs, laboratory maintenance, logistics, and so on, depending on the type of project. As the VBC evolves further, plans call for it to become an independent commercial entity such as a company limited by guarantee (registered as a non-profit organization).

## Case Study 2: University of Colombo

### Theekshana, University of Colombo School of Computing

The University of Colombo School of Computing (UCSC) has set up Theekshana as a provider of computing and software solutions to public entities, such as the Ministry of Foreign Affairs, Ministry of Finance, Sri Lanka Police, and Sri Lanka Army, and recently to an increasing number of private companies as well.

### Why Did Industry Partner with the University?

In the 1980s and 1990s, when computing solutions were limited, expertise in information and communication technologies (ICT) was available from several predecessor entities at the University of Colombo (UOC). This offered reliability and cost-effectiveness to industry while providing a learning experience to university students and faculty. After several successful partnerships with the government sector, more government agencies that were in need of special computing skills turned to the university, increasing the demand for its services. With the establishment of Theekshana in 2006, the university increased its competitive advantage by offering the best of both worlds: access to academic knowledge and resources coupled with the functionality and delivery system of a private company.

### What Did the University Gain from Working with Industry?

In developing computing solutions to industry-based problems, the staff and students of UCSC gained valuable learning experiences geared to practical application of learned knowledge. This helped establish UCSC as one of the top institutes in the country in ICT education. With the establishment of Theekshana, UCSC was able to generate profits to compensate the university as well as its employees. More employment and income-generating scenarios were open to students, staff, and the university. A public sector clientele adds value to UCSC as an institution by showcasing its industry-oriented learning and expertise and the reliability of services it provides.

### What Does It Take to Keep this University-Industry Partnership Successful?

At present, the sustainability of Theekshana depends solely on the higher management of UCSC, as the director of UCSC is also the chairman of the business entity. While the enthusiasm and proactive stance of management is key to sustaining successful university-industry partnerships, Theekshana also has to make sure that it attracts enough projects to have work on a continuous basis. It is currently making a major effort to market its services in order to counter private sector competitors that are aggressively marketing their own portfolios.

### How Did the Collaboration Start?

From the early 1980s, the UOC was involved in providing knowledge of and access to ICT, which were emerging rapidly in the developed countries. The Computing Services Centre (CSC), formed by the late Prof. V. K Samaranayake, served clients in industry and government that required computing services. One of its first projects was to provide support to the elections commissioner to conduct presidential and parliamentary elections, starting with the presidential elections of 1982. This project continues to the present and has become very complex, now that the electoral commissioner releases results not only to state media but also to other media and the Internet as well. Another early project was the development of software applications to display scorecards for cricket matches and other sports on Rupavahini, the national television network.

The CSC was attached to the Institute of Computer Technology when it was formed, and it was known as the Center for Computing in the late 1980s and early 1990s. At that time it served public and private clients as well as nongovernmental institutions such as Sarvodaya. Its clients include, among others, the Ministry of Foreign Affairs, Sri Lanka Police, Criminal Investigation Department, United Nations, Central Bank, Ministry of Finance, Department of Education, University Grants Commission, Julius & Creasy law firm, Rupavahini, Independent Television Network, Sri Lanka Broadcasting Corporation, and the Army and Navy.

When the Sri Lanka government established the Information and Communication Technology Agency (ICTA) in 2002–03, the stage was set for the further development of the ICT industry and for the formation of university companies in this field. Prof. Samaranayake envisioned university-associated companies that would be similar to those developed by major universities in the United States and the United Kingdom, where direct results of university research could be commercialized and expertise provided to end users through consultancies.

After much deliberation, Theekshana was set up in 2006, becoming one of only two nonprofit companies that were associated with public universities in Sri Lanka. Uni-Consultancy Services (UNIC) was formed by the University of Moratuwa with a similar vision but a larger scope, providing consultancy services in engineering as well as ICT.

### Key Stakeholders

At present, international and quasi-government organizations are the main stakeholders in Theekshana in addition to ICTA, which was the major stakeholder at the time Theekshana was incorporated. Through ICTA, the Sri Lanka Police, Ministry of Public Administration, Supreme Courts, and Ministry of Higher Education were initial stakeholders. The World Bank–funded projects IRQUE and HETC awarded several projects, and through these Theekshana provided solutions and services to universities and the University Grants Commission. Subsequently, the International Development Research Centre of Canada, the Royal University of Bhutan, and several private sector companies became stakeholders as well.

### The University-Industry Collaboration Unit

Theekshana was incorporated as a nonprofit limited liability company under the registrar of companies in Sri Lanka. It was formed as a society whose members are the permanent UCSC staff, and it is managed by UCSC. The director of UCSC by default becomes the chairman of Theekshana, and the heads of three departments of UCSC become ex-officio members of the Board, with two nominees from the UCSC Board.

At present, the chief operating officer of Theekshana is the head of the Software Development Unit of UCSC, who was involved in running Theekshana from its inception. Although Theekshana does not contribute directly to any academic programs at present, UCSC and UOC students undergo training at Theekshana annually for their six-month internships. Theekshana has earned profits in all years except 2006 and 2013 and has managed to accumulate more than SL Rs 10 million in reserves.

### Funding and Financial Management

Based upon Prof. Samaranayake's concept, Theekshana was incorporated in December 2006 with initial funding of SL Rs 100,000 from UCSC. This funding was used as seed money and was repaid two years later.

Theekshana is run on the same model that was developed at the time of incorporation, where its income is based upon the number of projects won by the company. The company retains 37 percent of the total value of projects for overhead. To make the company and its projects competitive in the market, the retention percentage in the formative years ranged from 10 percent to 30 percent, in addition to the retention for salaries in the salary fund. Consultants who are involved in projects are paid according to their contribution, and payment varies between 10 percent and 30 percent. If a project does not require assistants, this value could be higher due to the absence of a salary component. In some projects, only company retention has been kept, while the rest is absorbed by the relevant department or centers of UCSC. Theekshana pays rent to UCSC and also contributes to the UCSC Welfare Society.

### Resources

Theekshana obtains human resources from UCSC for most of its projects. As mentioned previously, senior staff acted as consultants or headed the majority of early projects. The entity also derived other resources from the university and obtained services from the Software Development Unit and E-Learning Centre, as well as other centers, for which appropriate payment was made.

Theekshana has contributed significantly to Sri Lanka as a foreign exchange earner through its projects for foreign clients and has provided expertise in the field of ICT, where other institutions do not have well-developed capabilities. It has made significant contributions to the Sri Lanka Police by developing the Automated Fingerprint Identification System (AFIS). This system would have cost the police more than a billion rupees if they had tried to purchase it on the international market. Theekshana has also developed several other systems, including a Birth, Marriage and Death Certificate Issuance System for Sri Lanka, as well as a university admissions system that is used by the UGC. Some of these projects have won several national awards.

As mentioned previously, Theekshana started its life without any capital and has survived up to now with stable growth and expansion thanks to the personal commitment of the people involved. Although Theekshana has made a significant contribution nationally, it has not been able to muster the full support of UCSC staff, for various reasons. It is clear that Theekshana will face major sustainability issues in the future.

In order for Theekshana to survive, certain provisions of the University Act need to be amended to allow UCSC or UOC to own companies, as do universities in Europe and North America. In addition, Theekshana must be able to market its services outside the UCSC umbrella. It has to be able to innovate, and it must be accepted by the UCSC community as one of their entities that will develop together with UCSC itself. The primary reason that Theekshana has sustainability challenges is the lack of understanding among the academic community in Sri Lanka of entrepreneurship and its essential element, risk taking. More broadly, it is widely assumed in Sri Lanka that any entrepreneurial venture or business can lead to mismanagement of financial resources, which may in turn lead to financial fraud. In some other countries, entrepreneurship is admired, and even failed efforts to start a business are highly regarded by society.

## Operational Model

The director of UCSC serves as the chairman of Theekshana, and the heads of three departments of UCSC are ex officio members of the Board, with two nominees from the UCSC Board. In addition, two members of the Theekshana Society are elected to represent members of the society at the annual general meeting for a year.

Theekshana appoints auditors at the annual general meeting as stipulated by the Registrar of Companies of Sri Lanka. In addition, Theekshana is presently audited by auditors of the UGC and the UOC, as well as government auditors. The senior assistant bursar acts as the chief accountant of the company.

## Experience Sharing

Theekshana has been used as a model for setting up several companies at UOC, including the Colombo Science and Technology Cell. Having identified some of the weaknesses of Theekshana, some staff members wanted to move away from the Theekshana model and suggested forming a private limited liability company in order to commercialize products of their research, with only a loose connection to UCSC.

The University of Kelaniya is also in the process of forming of a company similar to Theekshana.

## Constraints Faced during Implementation

When Theekshana was formed, it was not clear how it could find necessary capital, as no money was available for hiring of a manager or staff. Although UCSC could have provided additional funds, the University Act, applying to all universities in Sri Lanka, was silent as to whether such companies could be formed, let alone whether a university could provide funding for running a company.

During this critical period, Dr. Ruvan Weerasinghe, who succeeded the late Prof. Samarannayke as director of UCSC, requested that Mr. Harsha Wijayawardhana become chief technical officer of Theekshana, in addition to his responsibilities in running the Software Development Unit of UCSC. Mr. Wijayawardhana formulated a strategy by which he and others worked without pay during the formative period of Theekshana, until funding was secured. The first few projects undertaken by Theekshana were brought in by Mr. Wijayawardhana, Dr. Damith Karunarathne, and Dr. Weerasinghe. The first major project was the Birth, Marriage and Death Certificate Issuance System, a contract obtained by Mr. Wijayawardhana from ICTA based upon his automation projects carried out for the government of Sri Lanka.

Since Theekshana was without any funders or capital, Mr. Wijayawardhana suggested that profits from projects be retained in an emergency capital fund; this later grew to SL Rs 10 million. Most of profits from the Birth, Marriage and Death Certificate Issuance System were allocated to the emergency capital fund, becoming seed money for the fund. For an initial three-year period, during which Mr. Wijayawardhana worked to promote the company as chief operating officer and technical officer, he did not take any retainer fee, except for consultancy fees derived from the projects.

### Barriers to Sustainability

The following are some of barriers:

1. As mentioned previously, there is a lack of acceptance of Theekshana by UCSC staff.
2. Proper marketing has not been carried out.
3. Although staff can be permanent at Theekshana, the company still has only contract staff.
4. The company cannot move forward independently without going through highly bureaucratic red tape. One of the reasons for setting up the company was to avoid this problem, but the multiple audits by different entities have actually intensified it.

## Case Study 3: Wayamba University of Sri Lanka

### Department of Food Science and Technology

The Department of Food Science and Technology (DFST) at Wayamba University has developed an industrial partnership programme through its Innovation Center (IC). The creation of a laboratory with advanced technology to solve research and technology problems for the food industry is a key feature of the partnership.

### Why Did Industry Partner with the University?

The DFST at Wayamba University of Sri Lanka (WUSL) has developed a good reputation with industry for solving technical issues such as novel product development and shelf life determination, conducting regular tests, and providing technical expertise to them. Also, in order to obtain such services in research, industry needs to recruit competent graduates from the university as employees and carry out collaborative work with the university. Furthermore, industries partner with the university to train their personnel in handling laboratory equipment and conducting relevant operational procedures. Some of the industries are interested in collaborating with universities for the sake of recognition by society.

### What Value Did the University Add to Industry?

The DFST at WUSL prioritizes the needs of industrial partners and has developed an industrial partnership program. To cater to the needs of partner industries, DFST designs industrially important research using industrial inputs and develops innovative technologies that partner industries expect to reduce cost and wastage and utilize resources optimally. At the same time, the faculty visualizes the future needs of the nation and conducts innovations and product realization to benefit food industries. Therefore, relevant industries have benefited from customized innovations by the faculty and its students, suited for the respective sector. Two such examples are:

- Develop a methodology to export coconut apple preserve for a virgin coconut oil producer. Nutritional analysis and shelf life studies with different packaging formats are being conducted for this.
- Preserve and develop the color of tuna using permitted preservatives for a partner company that exports fish to Europe.

### What Did the University Gain from Working with Industry?
Industries are among the most important stakeholders of universities. The DFST conducts industrially important research after establishing a memorandum of understanding (MOU) with the respective industries. Hence industries fund the department's research programs. Furthermore, industries assist the department with their technical knowledge, enriching its expertise.

It is compulsory for students to obtain in-plant training and research experience to complete their degrees. During this training and research, industries provide the placements for the final-year undergraduates. Industrial experts provide a valuable contribution by mentoring undergraduates. Participation at career fairs and provision of job opportunities to DFST graduates is another gain. Industries also conduct guest lectures for undergraduates, offer practical training in the processing line, provide input in various situations (curriculum revision, etc.), and fund university events.

### What Does It Take to Keep this University-Industry Partnership Successful?
The department has an industrial membership program with food industries and conducts biannual meetings with industrial members. In supervising the final-year research of undergraduates, the department prioritizes the needs of partner industries and designs undergraduate research to resolve their technical issues. The establishment of an IC to satisfy industrial members is a key feature of this successful partnership with industry.

### What Can Other Universities Learn from this Case Study?
The creation of a laboratory with advanced technology to solve issues important to the food industry is a key feature of the partnership. In the biannual meetings, the industrial members provide fresh ideas and directions for the future activities of the Innovation Center (IC). The outreach program, with a Web-based approach designed and developed by the IC, also contributes to the success of this entity. It is hoped that other universities will understand the need to have sustainable partnerships with industries and will develop creative approaches to nurture a successful and sustainable university-industry partnership program, utilizing available resources.

### How Did the Collaboration Start?

The DFST has about 10 years of experience working with relevant industries, yet it needed to develop formal links with industries to have a sustainable relationship. With funds from the HETC Project for advancement of entities for research dissemination and commercialization (Quality and Innovation Grant, Window 4), the department introduced its industry collaborative arm, the IC, and attracted food industries by conducting an industrial awareness program. In this model, industries register for membership in the IC.

### Key Stakeholders

The key stakeholders are industrial partners (food industries), Wayamba University faculty, and Wayamba University undergraduates. The five key industrial partners currently working with the IC are Vetgrow, Ceylon Fisheries, Tropical Health Food Pvt. Ltd., Cowin Dairies, and Jandi Export Pvt. Ltd. Upon request, the IC works with other industries as well.

### The University-Industry Collaboration Unit

As stated earlier, the university-industry collaboration unit is called the Innovation Center. The coordinator of the IC, the head of the department, representative faculty members of the DFST, and industrial members provide the input to conduct the activities of the center. The IC has a technical panel comprising department faculty and two industrial experts who provide guidance on research design and help plan and prioritize future activities.

### Funding and Financial Management

The IC conducts activities and research as requested by industrial partners to solve their issues; therefore, the main financial contributors are the industrial members. Other forms of financial support include Wayamba University contributions, consortium membership fees, earnings from intellectual properties, training conducted by the center, and funding from the various projects. As the IC is an entity of Wayamba University, the university maintains control of its finances and administration, and the WUSL bursar manages the finances of the IC. The IC has conducted three programs in 2015, one of which is still ongoing. The total budget (from external sources) so far is just over SL Rs 1.5 million. The IC is expected to sign another MOU in 2015.

### Resources

Faculty, undergraduates, and industrial members are the most valued resources of the Innovation Centre. Furthermore, novel food products and technologies the IC has developed, and its ongoing research, are also resources of the center. The IC makes use of the physical resources of WUSL in conducting its activities. However, new laboratories have been developed with upgraded laboratory equipment to conduct industrially important research with funding from the HETC Quality and Innovation Grant, Window 4. Further, one industrial partner has sponsored an upgrading of a laboratory. Payments for the projects are done according to the MOU that is approved by university authorities.

### Operational Model

The IC provides services mainly to its members. Therefore, to obtain the services of the IC, the service recipient should have a membership in the IC. When a member communicates to the coordinator of the IC its intention to conduct an industrially important research project, the coordinator directs the request to expert faculty members and a project proposal is developed. The proposal is then directed to the Technical Panel of the IC, and inputs are gained from a multidisciplinary group. Thereafter, it is directed to the respective industrial member and a MOU is developed, including inputs from both university and industry. Once the MOU is signed by the university and the industrial member, the research can proceed under the terms and conditions stated in the agreement. While the IC is flexible with respect to the conditions in the MOU, a fair share of the projected income is retained for the university. The terms and conditions are discussed with the DFST team as well as with the industrial partner, and an agreement is reached. Therefore, terms, conditions, and intellectual property rights (IPR) vary from one agreement to another. Budget lines are developed by following University Council–approved guidelines and considering the actual cost.

During the biannual meeting of the consortium, progress on the ongoing projects and research are presented to industrial members. All industrial partners (five at present) are invited to the biannual meetings. Furthermore, the IC attempts to attract companies in its vicinity to obtain membership. Thus, a few companies (about five) are made aware of the IC activities and encouraged to become IC members. During the sessions, members can present their opinions, expectations, and needs. With input from the industrial members, faculty members can develop a project proposal and it can be implemented through the IC.

Presently, industrial partners do not use laboratories at the department, but the IC is willing to let them work in the laboratories in the future, under the supervision of the IC.

If an industry is interested in obtaining test services and training from the IC, the respective industry is expected to communicate with the coordinator, stating the requirement. The IC will then conduct the training or test service expected by the industry. So far the IC has had one year of experience in this process, and three training sessions have been conducted for the partners during this year.

If a project initiated by a faculty member or student has an outcome, it is shared with the contributors according to the proportion of their contribution. This is one of the governing norms of the IC of WUSL.

### Experience Sharing

The IC maintains confidentiality and respects the terms of agreements made with the membership. For the development of the food industry and start-up companies, the IC is quite generous and shares its expertise and experience for the benefit of the whole nation. Concept foods and technologies developed by the IC are being commercialized and are key attractions of membership.

Most recently, the IC has developed novel technologies and concept foods such as a "silver tip" tea development alternative methodology, Ayurvedic carbonated beverages, coconut apple preserve, organic pineapple vinegar, carrot yogurt, and technology to preserve scraped coconut. These developments are some of the key attractions of the center. Hence, the IC is interested in sharing the outcome with other universities and industries without creating any conflict of interest and without breaching agreements with the industrial partners. Patents and IPR for the industrially funded projects are implemented according to the clauses in the MOU.

## Case Study 4: University of Moratuwa

Moratuwa University has established several long-term partnerships with companies. Three examples are presented here: (a) the Electronic Systems Research Laboratory, developed in partnership with Zone24×7, a software company headquartered in California; (b) the Rubber Product and Process Development Incubator, developed with the DSI Samson Group; and (c) the Mobile Communication Research Laboratory, developed with Dialog Axiata, the largest telecommunication service provider in Sri Lanka.

### Zone24×7 and Electronic Systems Research Laboratory
#### Why Did Industry Partner with the University?
Zone24×7 Inc., the sponsor of the laboratory, is a leading provider of global technology innovation services, headquartered in San Jose, California. Zone24×7 develops and deploys mission-critical, cost-effective, quality enterprise products and solutions. The company has been recognized as a Microsoft Gold Certified Partner in Mobility Solutions, Custom Development Solutions, and Data Management Solutions, and also a Microsoft Gold Partner in Embedded Solutions. Zone24×7 has technology development centers in the United States, Malaysia, and Sri Lanka. Guided by the vision "Research Locally, Apply Globally," Zone24×7 established the research laboratory with UOM to help local researchers achieve global recognition.

#### What Value Did the University Add to Industry?
The University of Moratuwa produces top graduates who demonstrate a high research potential. The Department of Electronic and Telecommunication Engineering at UOM offers a BSc engineering degree course, two postgraduate diploma/master of engineering courses, and a full-time postgraduate research program. The popularity of the department's undergraduate program is so high that only those undergraduates with a grade point average over 3.8 in the common and competitive first year can enter the program. The department is well known for the quality of the graduates it produces, and as a result there is strong

demand from both industry and academia worldwide for its graduates. Therefore the department is continuing to forge strong links with industry in order to promote collaborative research and product development work. The researchers in the laboratory can benefit from a high-quality work and research environment with state-of-the-art equipment while receiving research advice from the department's faculty and expertise from the Zone24×7 parent company. Some research students choose to follow a MSc program at the department as well, and some of them have secured admission to prestigious graduate schools such as Johns Hopkins University.

### What Did the University Gain from Working with Industry?

The joint lab research will enable the students and researchers involved to lead the next generation of innovation in diversified business domains. The main emphasis is to develop the research competencies of the students while focusing on research work that will enable future advancements. The research laboratory strives to highlight the presence of Sri Lanka on the map by carrying out world-class research at the Department of Electronic and Telecommunication Engineering.

### What Does It Take to Keep this University-Industry Partnership Successful?

Funding to attract graduates who have the best research and development potential is critical. Also important is reaching an understanding among key stakeholders about the ups and downs of volatile business environments.

### How Did the Collaboration Start?

The University of Moratuwa had always sought to forge strong links with industry in order to promote collaborative research and product development work. Zone24×7 Pvt. Ltd. had been interacting with the department for some time, supporting undergraduate projects. The university learned that the products developed by the company are trusted by industry leaders, including Federated Department Stores, Symbol Technologies, Motorola, Posiflex, and ID Tech in the United States, and RDM Corporation in Canada. During these interactions both parties felt that the level of engagement could be raised to become more mutually beneficial by establishing a research collaboration in the form of a laboratory, so that graduates could be retained to contribute to innovative product development by doing its research component while remaining in an academic environment. Discussions were initiated and proceeded until the laboratory was established. The research lab was declared open by the U.S. ambassador to Sri Lanka and Maldives on September 6, 2007, at an inauguration ceremony attended by the chancellor of the university, faculty members, and industry leaders.

### Resources, Financial Management, and Operational Model

Senior staff of the Department of Electronic and Telecommunication Engineering and Zone24×7 have acted as research advisers and consultants for the research projects. The physical location is provided by the university within the department premises. Equipment and furniture were provided by Zone24×7, as well as networking and teleconferencing facilities and the virtual interface with the Software Product Development Environment. Zone24×7 also provided funding for the research students.

Activities of the research laboratory are overseen by a Board of Management consisting of the head of the Department of Electronic and Telecommunication Engineering, the general manager of Zone24×7, and the director of the laboratory.

### Experience Sharing

In addition to disseminating its work through several publications, the laboratory has carried out national projects. In these cases it supported local government requirements and developed solutions at their request free of charge, as a national obligation. These projects were carried out jointly by the undergraduates under the guidance and supervision of the academic staff and experienced senior product developers of Zone24×7. Some examples are:

- A vehicle management system for the Finance Ministry proposed by the Management Audit Department, Ministry of Finance and Planning, to automate the handling of state-owned vehicles using a Web-based system.
- An accident data management system proposed by the Police Department and World Health Organization for recoding details of accidents in Sri Lanka and performing statistical analysis and modeling to support accident management and traffic planning at the national level.

Furthermore, there has been strong support from the company's experienced product developers for undergraduate mini-projects and projects for developing the skills of our undergraduates through the research laboratory. This has been very beneficial for our undergraduates.

### Barriers to Sustainability

1. Insufficient funding to keep good research students. Funding is very difficult at times when the partner company experiences business downturns.
2. High demand for graduates in industry and academia, both locally and internationally. They get very attractive offers and leave. It is extremely difficult to keep them in Sri Lanka without proper compensation.
3. Lack of appreciation from the government organization for the hard work done by the undergraduates through the laboratory to fulfill national obligations. This really discourages student involvement in such challenging projects.

## SIL-UOM Rubber Products and Process Development Incubator
### Why Did Industry Partner with the University?

The Sri Lankan rubber products industry needs to continuously introduce high-quality, cost-competitive products and novel technologies. R&D activity, aimed at being first to market with better products, has become a matter of survival. The new challenge for industrial R&D organizations is to accelerate the product development process. The industry wants to discover and create new products and technologies that will result in revolutionary changes, and to make them a little faster than anybody else does.

### What Value Did the University Add to Industry?

The industry receives answers to problems that it is not equipped to resolve on its own, drawing on the multidisciplinary expertise available at the university. Working with the academic community exposes industrial researchers to new research trends, advanced technical and analytical approaches, and novel experimental techniques.

The huge improvements in process and development of new products, driven by new technologies, are helping the industry meet the challenges of the price-competitive and quality-conscious global market. Productivity improvements through reducing waste and reclaiming and recycling process waste in the industry are increasingly important in sustaining the natural environment, and the key role of science and technological innovation in this area is greatly beneficial.

### What Did the University Gain from Working with Industry?

The university gains assistance in upgrading and maintaining laboratories connected with the incubator, and more recognition from society and funding agencies. By working on incubator projects, knowledge workers of the university entering the workforce gain greater and early exposure to marketing, manufacturing, processes, and environmental concerns, in addition to technology transfer. All are factors of great importance to industry. Involvement in incubator projects will provide additional income to the technical staff of the university.

Undergraduates and postgraduates have opportunities to conduct their research in an industrial environment under the guidance of academics and industry consultants, and with a supply of raw materials that are not freely available on the local market. New graduates have the opportunity to seek employment in the DSI Samson Group of industries, without much waiting time after graduation.

### What Does It Take to Keep this University-Industry Partnership Successful?

As a result of the partnership, a considerable number of projects have been handled by the incubator since its establishment. Some of the projects are based on cost reduction, to make products competitive in global market, and on quality improvement, so that they meet international standards. Others focus on process developments to enhance productivity and utilize energy and other resources effectively and economically. All these projects help to diversify the product portfolio of Samson International PLC (SIL). Certain products developed by the incubator have been commercialized successfully at SIL.

The guidance provided for the incubator projects from both university academics and industry consultants will be essential to the successful completion of the projects. Another major factor is the monitoring mechanism implemented for operation of the projects.

### How Did the Collaboration Start?

The University of Moratuwa offers several study programs related to the rubber industry: a BSc engineering degree in chemical and process engineering with a focus area in polymer engineering; a national diploma in polymer technology; an MSc/PG diploma in polymer technology (part-time basis); and a certificate in polymer technology (part-time basis). It has catered to the polymer industry since the 1980s. The Department of Chemical and Process Engineering (DCPE) has established long-term collaborations with the rubber industry, especially through these study programs. DCPE is equipped with highly qualified academics who hold PhD degrees from world-renowned universities and have long-term industrial experience.

To be competitive in the global market, most rubber products manufacturing industries have understood that their R&D facility would not be able to handle specific research projects, especially on innovation processes, due to an inadequate knowledge base and commitment to such projects with ongoing production capacities. There are practical difficulties and high costs involved in setting up a fully equipped R&D facility in the industry.

Industrial-academic research partnerships have become an important part of corporate R&D. Several basic trends have fueled these links and were made possible through the concept of the technology incubator. The government also offers tax benefits for industrial-academic research partnerships.

SIL, a subsidiary company of the DSI Samson Group, is one of the largest rubber products manufacturers and exporters in Sri Lanka. Building on the long-term relationship between academics at DCPE and personnel at DSI Samson, the SIL-UOM Rubber Products and Process Development Incubator was established in February 2011. It also built on the technology incubator concept, which had been introduced at the University of Moratuwa for the first time when it established the Dialog lab (see below).

The rubber products incubator was set up under an agreement between SIL, Samson Compounds Pvt. Ltd. (SCOM), UOM, and UNIC to carry out joint research and development. Areas of activity are as follows:

- To come up with a plausible design for the scale-up of selected products
- To develop a commercially viable product or process on a laboratory scale
- To develop new recipes and processes to make existing products competitive in the market
- To improve the efficiency of machinery and equipment that are being used at present
- To improve the process with the target of reducing the rejection rate
- To reduce and conserve the energy consumed in the process
- To find the means of sourcing of new technologies and make recommendations for introduction of new value-added products

### The University-Industry Collaboration Unit

The SIL-UOM Rubber Products and Process Development Incubator does not contribute directly to any academic program at present. However, a significant number of undergraduate and postgraduate research projects are funded by the incubator. Fresh graduates have the opportunity to join the incubator and SCOM, SIL, or DSI, while the in-plant trainees have the opportunity to carry out their training.

Most of the rubber processing equipment at the polymer processing laboratory of the department, which was nonoperational for long time, has been repaired. The facilities are now available for undergraduate and postgraduate research work. The laboratory is being maintained under the incubator budget.

With this collaboration, under the public-private grant scheme, a National Research Council grant was obtained to offer a PhD degree program. Two National Science Foundation grants were also obtained: one to set up a biodegradable testing facility at the department and one to fabricate a compression mould to produce foam rubber sheets continuously at SIL.

### Funding and Financial Management

Fifty percent of the funding for the project will be provided by SIL and SCOM; these funds will be specifically utilized for the design, management, and implementation of the project. The UOM contribution will cover the balance, 50 percent of the project cost. The laboratory equipment and furniture will be jointly owned by UOM and SIL/SCOM and will be located at UOM during the project. On completion of the project, SIL/SCOM equipment will be donated to UOM.

UNIC is responsible for administration of the finances and is accountable to the Board of Management. UNIC will charge 15 percent of the budget (excluding the budget for capital equipment) as an administrative and financial management fee. SIL, SCOM, and UOM and the Board are entitled to inspect the books of accounts or project ledgers and any other documentation relating to disbursements of the finances related to the project.

SIL/SCOM has the right to commercialize and utilize the collaboration technology. SIL/SCOM will pay UOM 5 percent of the net sales derived from such commercialization.

### Resources

The SIL-UOM Rubber Products and Process Development Incubator obtains its human resources from all departments at UOM for most of its projects. Senior academics from various disciplines serve as research advisers and provide guidance to the research team of the incubator until the successful completion of projects, while technical staff provide their services to overcome technical problems encountered.

Processing, testing, and analytical equipment available at the DCPE and other departments is utilized. Online access to most of the scientific publications that are not frequently available to the industry is also a key resource for the incubator.

## Operational Model

The Board of Management is the supreme authority on all matters relating to all aspects of the project. The Board consists of three members nominated by the managing director of SIL, two members nominated by the vice chancellor of UOM, and one member nominated by the chairman of UNIC. The Board provides overall direction for the project by developing and supervising the implementation of plans and strategies, including evaluation and approval of new proposals. The Board meets every three months.

The Committee of Operations meets every month. The director of process incubator has overall responsibility for implementation of the activities of the incubator in accordance with the plans and strategies circulated by the Board. The director of projects is a full-time employee of the incubator and is responsible for training of personnel, project formulation, management and documentation, and market analysis.

The functions of the Committee of Operations include selection of projects (short term and long term) based on their priority, submission of comprehensive proposals to the Board for approval, monitoring the progress of projects, reporting the progress to top management, and day-to-day operations of the projects. Industry expectations are quite high, due to the need to produce commercially viable products and develop new processes.

## Barriers to Sustainability

The main challenges are:

- The need to complete the targeted projects within the given time frame, alongside the routine academic, research, and administrative workload of the academics from various disciplines
- The need to source new materials within a short period of time
- High R&D costs associated with testing carried out by accredited laboratories, locally and internationally

Barriers to the success of the incubator are:

- Lack of a proper marketing arm operated by the industry to market novel products developed by the incubator
- The struggle to retain young graduates who are recruited on contract basis with limited benefits to work at the incubator

## Dialog–University of Moratuwa Mobile Communications Research Laboratory
### Why Did Industry Partner with the University?

The intention was to explore innovations in mobile/Internet applications and services.

*What Value Did the University Add to Industry?*
The university is able to provide expertise, time, and people for the industry to explore new ideas.

*What Did the University Gain from Working with Industry?*
- Exposure to industry processes related to product development and deployment and/or commercialization
- Exposure to how industry looks at technology/design criteria in terms of business issues and use cases
- Access to telecommunications network infrastructure and a user base for research and development
- Opportunity to recruit full-time research personnel
- Opportunity to support, financially and technically, advanced undergraduate projects and a limited number of postgraduate research projects

*What does it take to keep this university-industry partnership successful?*
- Close collaboration and a good relationship between the two partners at the engineering level, with continuous dialog and progress monitoring of work
- Support and interest of higher management of the industry partner
- Commitment from the university to manage the lab
- Flexibility in day-to-day operations

*How Did the Collaboration Start?*
A large number of graduates of the Department of Electronic and Telecommunication Engineering have been recruited by Dialog Axiata PLC as engineers since the early 1990s. Arising from this, the department has a long history of close collaboration with Dialog Axiata PLC. Many ideas for undergraduate projects, resource provision, as well as collaborative supervision of projects were happening informally over a long period of time. The establishment of the Dialog–University of Moratuwa Mobile Communications Research Laboratory was an effort to strengthen and formalize this collaboration.

*Funding and Financial Management*
The lab is fully funded by Dialog Axiata PLC, based on a tripartite agreement between the University of Moratuwa, Dialog, and UNIC. The laboratory's financial management is carried out by UNIC, which employs the lab's research engineers and purchases equipment and other supplies on behalf of the lab.

UNIC is an association affiliated with the academic staff of the University of Moratuwa. It is registered under the Sri Lanka Companies Act No. 07 of 2007 as a company limited by guarantee, carrying on its business at the University of Moratuwa. It is the commercial arm of the university and acts as a "facilitator" for university-industry interactions. UNIC is managed by a board of managers consisting of the top management of the University of Moratuwa.

### Operational Model
The legal framework of the lab is established and functions under the above-mentioned tripartite agreement. The composition of the Board of Management is as follows:

- Three members nominated by the director/chief executive officer of Dialog
- One member from Dialog's holding company, Axiata Group Berhad Malaysia, nominated by Dialog
- Four members nominated by UOM, comprising the dean of the engineering faculty or nominee; the head of the Department of Computer Science and Engineering; the head of the Department of Electronic and Telecommunication Engineering; and one person nominated by the head of the Department of Electronic and Telecommunications Engineering to be appointed by the Council of the UOM as the director of the laboratory

The Board meets at least once every three months to evaluate the operations of the laboratory. The lab is subjected to the auditing procedure of UNIC.

From the University of Moratuwa, a member of the academic staff appointed as director of the laboratory is responsible for its management. The director has the overall responsibility for planning and implementing activities of the lab in order to guide it toward its long-term objectives. The director also coordinates technical, financial, and managerial functions between the laboratory, Dialog, UOM, and UNIC. Other members of the academic staff participate as research advisers, depending on their availability and interest in ongoing projects.

From Dialog, the chief coordinator is the head of the New Product and Service Innovation Division. Management of projects is carried out by an Operations Committee consisting of senior research engineers in the lab and personnel of the New Product and Service Innovation Division of Dialog.

The Operations Committee holds monthly progress review meetings. In addition, quarterly meetings are held with the lab's research personnel, members of the New Product and Service Innovation Division, and the senior management of Dialog to discuss and decide on directions for ongoing projects and initiation of new projects.

### Experience Sharing
The Dialog–University of Moratuwa Mobile Communications Research Laboratory is the first-ever industry-sponsored lab to be set up in the Sri Lankan higher education system. The agreement for its establishment was developed over nine months of discussions between the senior management and legal division of Dialog and the Council of the University of Moratuwa. It has been used as a model for setting up a number of labs along similar lines at the UOM.

The lab's work has resulted in two patents, with Dialog and the University of Moratuwa (and a third company in one case) as joint owners. Its products have won recognition at many national, regional, and international forums.

The lab has found that having UNIC as the financial manager enables it to function relatively independently with respect to recruitment of personnel and procurement.

### Constraints Faced during Implementation

- The lab's work is strongly biased toward innovations in electronics design. The support for mass production of electronics products locally was quite poor until recently. However, lately many facilities have emerged to fill this gap.
- Dialog's internal company processes do not provide much support for taking up innovations developed in the lab, due to concerns related to maintenance and upgrading. Processes had to be evolved to transfer the outcomes to Dialog for actual implementation.
- The reluctance to take risks that characterizes the telecommunications industry in general is a barrier to free innovation in the field.
- Research projects undertaken by the lab are usually relatively short-term and are of an applied nature. Such projects in general are not suited to be considered for postgraduate research degrees, though there are exceptions.
- There is a lack of active participation by academic staff members, other than the director, due to the academic workload and the above-mentioned nature of projects.
- The lack of a clear career path for research personnel has been a demotivating factor, though salaries are competitive with industry.

# 2015 Survey Methodology and Questionnaires

Two separate structured questionnaires were developed for universities and industry. The questionnaires were hosted on the Higher Education for the Twenty First Century (HETC) Project website, and e-mails were sent out to individuals identified as potential respondents, inviting them to participate.

All 15 national universities were covered by the survey. The target group within the universities consisted of deans, heads of departments, directors of centers and units, and senior faculty members.

In the absence of a complete sample framework for industries from which to draw a random sample, company contacts were obtained from multiple sources, including industry contact lists obtained from universities, HETC industry contacts, MBA alumni directories, and personal contacts of the research team. The survey was aimed at chief executive officers and senior management of the companies.

The survey was open for two months, from July to August 2015. After three rounds of reminders, 191 questionnaires from universities and 85 questionnaires from industry were returned. For the purpose of the analysis, 165 university questionnaire responses and 80 industry questionnaire responses were considered. Only one complete response was considered for each university department, unit, or center. In cases where more than one questionnaire was returned by the same department/unit/center, one was chosen for inclusion based on the following priority ranking: head, director, unit head, senior academic staff member. Duplicate questionnaires for the same department/unit/center, as well as several incomplete questionnaires, were excluded.

The 2015 data were compared with data from a study carried out in 2007 by a member of the current team. The 2007 survey covered 46 university departments and 36 companies, a much smaller sample than in 2015. To enhance comparability, the analysis sometimes breaks out separately the 2015 data for university departments in disciplines corresponding to those that responded to the 2007 survey. In tables where this is done, 2015a represents all 2015 data, and 2015b represents data that correspond to disciplines represented in the 2007 study.

## Questionnaire for Industry

### Study on Current Status of University-Industry Collaboration in Sri Lanka

1. Name of your company:

2. Your designation:
   CEO
   GM
   Head of Department/Division
   Senior Manager
   Junior Manager

3. Address and company website:

4. The main sector in which you do business?
   Manufacturing
   Trading
   Service
   Construction
   Information technology
   Others, please specify:

5. Legal status of your company?
   Public listed
   Private limited liability
   Partnership
   Sole proprietorship
   State corporation
   Others, please specify:

6. Total number of employees in your company (as of 30 June 2015):
   Number of employees

7. Annual turnover of your company (in Sri Lanka rupees):
   Less than 1 million
   Less than 10 million
   Less than 20 million
   Less than 50 million
   Less than 100 million
   Less than 500 million
   More than 500 million

8. What types of links does your company have with universities?
   Personal contacts with university academics
   Attendance at seminars, symposiums, workshops, and conferences
   Attendance at training programmes
   Providing university student internships
   Exchange of information, literature, data, etc. with university academics

Use of laboratory facilities belonging to universities
Engage university academic staff for consultancy
Engage university academic staff for contract research
Conduct joint research with university academics
Engage university academic staff in projects
Use university-held patents
Involve in joint curriculum development
Involve in development of spin-off companies
Others, please specify:

9. Do you think universities should engage in R&D (research and development) activities with industry?
Yes
Indifferent
No
Don't know

10. How useful would collaboration with universities be for your company?
1 – highly useful, 2 – useful, 3 – moderately useful, 4 – not useful

|  | 1 | 2 | 3 | 4 |
|---|---|---|---|---|
| 1. Obtain access to new ideas and know-how |  |  |  |  |
| 2. Useful for new product and process development |  |  |  |  |
| 3. Useful for product and process improvement |  |  |  |  |
| 4. Useful for quality improvement of the company |  |  |  |  |
| 5. Useful for solving technical problems |  |  |  |  |
| 6. Recruit high-quality graduates |  |  |  |  |
| 7. Reduce in-house R&D (research and development) cost |  |  |  |  |
| 8. Useful for continuing education of our staff |  |  |  |  |
| Others, please specify: |  |  |  |  |
| Others, please specify: |  |  |  |  |
| Others, please specify: |  |  |  |  |

11. Does your company have a section/unit/division/department devoted to R&D?
Yes
No

12. What percentage of your annual turnover is utilized for R&D?
Less than 0.5%
Less than 1%
Less than 5%
More than 5%

13. If your company has successful collaboration with a university, what are the success factors?

14. Constraints on university-industry interactions. Please indicate to what extent the following factors prevent your company from interacting with universities.

1 – very great extent, 2 – great extent, 3 – somewhat, 4 – very little, 5 – not at all

|  | 1 | 2 | 3 | 4 | 5 |
|---|---|---|---|---|---|
| 1. Differences between the universities and my company in values, mission, or priorities (e.g., academia vs. corporate values) |  |  |  |  |  |
| 2. Academics are not competent enough to undertake consultancy/industry-oriented research |  |  |  |  |  |
| 3. Lack of motivation among academics |  |  |  |  |  |
| 4. Lack of entrepreneurial spirit among academics |  |  |  |  |  |
| 5. Low commercialization potential of university research |  |  |  |  |  |
| 6. There are no proper mechanisms to collaborate with universities |  |  |  |  |  |
| 7. Poor communication between the universities and us |  |  |  |  |  |
| 8. Most universities lack adequate research facilities |  |  |  |  |  |
| 9. Universities are not interested in collaborating with us |  |  |  |  |  |
| 10. We are not aware of expertise/facilities available at universities |  |  |  |  |  |
| 11. We don't know whom to contact at universities to initiate collaborative activities |  |  |  |  |  |
| 12. Our business is not big enough to seek assistance from universities |  |  |  |  |  |
| 13. Lack of funds to initiate collaborative work with universities |  |  |  |  |  |
| 14. The university structure is not adapted to the needs of industrial collaborations |  |  |  |  |  |
| 15. Lack of clear IPR rules for U-I collaboration |  |  |  |  |  |
| 16. Geographical location of our facilities results in less access to universities |  |  |  |  |  |
| Others, please specify |  |  |  |  |  |
| Others, please specify |  |  |  |  |  |

15. Suggestions for improving university-industry interactions. Please indicate the effectiveness of the following measures for improving interaction between university and industry.

1 – not at all effective, 2 – slightly effective, 3 – effective, 4 – very effective

|  | 1 | 2 | 3 | 4 |
|---|---|---|---|---|
| 1. Include industrial internship in the curricula |  |  |  |  |
| 2. Encourage industrial visits by students |  |  |  |  |
| 3. Encourage regular industrial visits by academics |  |  |  |  |
| 4. Improve laboratory facilities and other infrastructure at universities |  |  |  |  |
| 5. Involve staff from industry in teaching programmes |  |  |  |  |
| 6. Publicize university activities relevant to industry |  |  |  |  |
| 7. Jointly (university and industry) organize informal meetings, talks, communications |  |  |  |  |
| 8. Government tax concessions for companies collaborating with universities |  |  |  |  |
| 9. Set up industrial parks closer to universities |  |  |  |  |
| 10. Encourage academic representation in industrial committees/chambers/boards |  |  |  |  |
| 11. Encourage industry representation in university committees |  |  |  |  |
| 12. Make available public seed money to foster U-I R&D collaboration |  |  |  |  |
| Others, please specify: |  |  |  |  |
| Others, please specify: |  |  |  |  |
| Others, please specify: |  |  |  |  |

16. Do you have any other suggestions for improving university-industry collaborations?

Yes

No

If yes, please state suggestions:

If no, please state why:

## Questionnaire for Universities

### Study on Current Status of University-Industry Collaboration in Sri Lanka

1. Name of the university:

2. Faculty:

3. Department/Unit/Center:

4. Number of students in the faculty:

5. Designation of the respondent:
   Dean
   Head of the department
   Director of unit/center
   Professor
   Senior lecturer
   Lecturer

6. Total number of academic staff in the department/unit/center:
   Professor
   Senior lecturer
   Lecturer
   Technical officer
   Administrative officer

7. Did your department/unit/center receive any funds from the following sources during the past two years:
   Industry (private)
   Industry (public)
   Private foundations
   International funding agencies
   NGOs
   Others, please specify:

8. Please describe the laboratory facilities at your department/unit/center. The laboratory facilities are:
   Adequate for teaching
   Inadequate for teaching
   Adequate for research
   Inadequate for research

9. Does your department/unit/center collaborate with industry?
   Yes
   No

10. If yes, what types of collaboration exist between your department/unit/center and industry?
    Research consultancy
    Industrial placements

Resource and knowledge sharing
Patents/licensing
Spin-offs

11. What services/facilities are offered by your department/unit/center to industry?
Consultancy
Contract research
Joint research
Training company employees
Postgraduate training
Workshops
Seminars
Laboratory facilities
University patents
Prototypes developed by you
Others, please specify

12. Does your university have an industry liaison office/university-industry interaction unit?
Yes
No

13. Has your department/unit/center undertaken any collaborative research and development/consultancy projects during the past two years with the following:
Industry (private)
Industry (public)
Private foundations
International agencies
NGOs
Others, please specify:

14. What is the approximate value of monetary resources involved in the U-I collaborations with the following?
Industry (private)
Industry (public)
Private foundations
International agencies
NGOs
Others, please specify:

15. How many research proposals/consultancy/project reports were submitted to the following by your department/unit/center during the past two years?
Industry (private)
Industry (public)
Private foundations
International agencies
NGOs
Others, please specify:

16. How many spin-off companies (companies set up by academics, researchers, students, and graduates in order to commercially use the outcomes of the research in which they were involved at the university) has your department/unit/center supported in the last two years?

17. Your department/unit collaboration with industry was coordinated by:
Individually
Through U-I interaction unit
Research team
Dean/head of department
NGO
Others, please specify:

18. If your department/unit/center had successful collaboration with industry, what were the success factors?

19. Constraints on university-industry collaboration. Please indicate to what extent the following factors prevent your department/unit/center from interacting with industry.
1 – very great extent, 2 – great extent, 3 – somewhat, 4 – very little, 5 – not at all

|  | 1 | 2 | 3 | 4 | 5 |
|---|---|---|---|---|---|
| 1. Our research capabilities are not relevant to the industry |  |  |  |  |  |
| 2. Academics do not feel confident enough to undertake industry-oriented research |  |  |  |  |  |
| 3. Lack of motivation among faculty |  |  |  |  |  |
| 4. Lack of entrepreneurial spirit among faculty |  |  |  |  |  |
| 5. Time constraint due to heavy teaching and administrative workload |  |  |  |  |  |
| 6. It is not the mission of the academic researcher to collaborate with industry |  |  |  |  |  |
| 7. Academics are not aware of the possible channels for getting sponsored research and consultancy assignments |  |  |  |  |  |
| 8. Collaboration with industry has a negative influence on the pedagogic mission of a university |  |  |  |  |  |
| 9. Industry is not interested to collaborate with universities |  |  |  |  |  |
| 10. Collaboration with industry limits the free choice of research topics |  |  |  |  |  |

| | | | | | |
|---|---|---|---|---|---|
| 11. Inadequate infrastructure (communication, transport, journals, books) | | | | | |
| 12. Inadequate laboratory facilities | | | | | |
| 13. Lack of autonomy to work with industry | | | | | |
| 14. The university structure is not adapted to the needs of industrial collaborations | | | | | |
| 15. University norms and procedures hamper collaboration with industry | | | | | |
| 16. The university has no policy toward collaborations with industry | | | | | |
| 17. Geographical location of the university results in less access to industry | | | | | |
| 18. Lack of clear IPR rules for U-I collaboration | | | | | |
| Others, please specify: | | | | | |
| Others, please specify: | | | | | |
| Others, please specify: | | | | | |

20. Suggestions for improving university-industry interactions. Please indicate the effectiveness of following measures for improving interaction between university and industry.

1 – not at all effective, 2 – slightly effective, 3 – effective, 4 – very effective

| | 1 | 2 | 3 | 4 |
|---|---|---|---|---|
| 1. Include industrial internship in the curricula | | | | |
| 2. Encourage industrial visits by students | | | | |
| 3. Encourage regular industrial visits by faculty | | | | |
| 4. Improve laboratory facilities | | | | |
| 5. Involve staff from industry in teaching programmes | | | | |
| 6. Set up U-I interaction cells in universities | | | | |
| 7. Publicize university activities relevant to industry | | | | |
| 8. Conduct seminars, workshops for staff from industry | | | | |
| 9. Provide tax concessions for companies collaborating with universities | | | | |
| 10. Make it obligatory for academics to undertake a certain amount of work with industry | | | | |
| 11. Use industry collaboration as a criteria for salary increments and promotions of academics | | | | |
| 12. Give more autonomy for academics to work with industry | | | | |
| 13. Make available public seed money to foster U-I R&D collaboration | | | | |

| | | | | |
|---|---|---|---|---|
| 14. Formulate clear rules for universities to generate and retain revenues from U-I collaboration | | | | |
| Others, please specify: | | | | |
| Others, please specify: | | | | |
| Others, please specify: | | | | |
| Others, please specify: | | | | |

21. Do you have any other suggestions for improving university-industry collaborations?

Yes

No

If yes, please state suggestions:

If no, please state why:

# Workshop on Promoting University-Industry Collaborations in Sri Lanka

January 19, 2016, Hotel Galadari, Lotus Road, Colombo

**Agenda**

8:30 a.m.–9:00 a.m.
Registration

9:00 a.m.–9:40 a.m.
Welcome address
      Prof. P. S. M. Gunaratne, Director, HETC Project

Additional remarks
      Hon. Lakshman Kiriella, Minister of Higher Education and Highways
      Hon. Mohan Lal Grero, State Minister of Higher Education
      Prof. Mohan de Silva, Chairman, University Grants Commission
      Prof. Sirimali Fernando, Chief Executive Officer, COSTI
      Mr. Sanjeewa Gunawardena, Chief Executive Officer, Darley Butler & Co. Limited
      Mrs. Françoise Clottes, Country Director for Sri Lanka and the Maldives, World Bank

9:40 a.m.–10:00 a.m.
Presentation of draft report on "Promoting University-Industry Collaboration in Sri Lanka: Status, Case Studies, and Policy Options"
      Dr. Kurt Larsen, Senior Education Specialist, World Bank
      Prof. Deepthi Bandara, Deputy Director, HETC Project

10:00 a.m.–11:00 a.m.
University-Industry Collaboration: Case Studies

> University of Moratuwa, presented by Prof. Ananda Jayawardene, Vice Chancellor, University of Moratuwa
>
> Theekshana, University of Colombo School of Computing, presented by Mr. Harsha Wijewardene, CTO Theekshana
>
> Innovation Center, Wayamba University, presented by Mr. Danesh Liyanage, Faculty of Livestock, Fisheries and Nutrition, Wayamba University of Sri Lanka
>
> Veterinary Business Center, University of Peradeniya, presented by Dr. L. J. P. A. P. Jayasooriya, Faculty of Veterinary Medicine and Animal Science, University of Peradeniya

11:00 a.m.–11:15 a.m.
Tea and coffee break

11:15 a.m.–12:00 p.m.
"Way Forward": Working group session

12:00 p.m.–1:15 p.m.
Plenary: Feedback from working groups and discussion

1:15 p.m.–1:30 p.m.
Conclusion

1:30 p.m.–2:30 p.m.
Lunch

**Environmental Benefits Statement**

The World Bank Group is committed to reducing its environmental footprint. In support of this commitment, the Publishing and Knowledge Division leverages electronic publishing options and print-on-demand technology, which is located in regional hubs worldwide. Together, these initiatives enable print runs to be lowered and shipping distances decreased, resulting in reduced paper consumption, chemical use, greenhouse gas emissions, and waste.

The Publishing and Knowledge Division follows the recommended standards for paper use set by the Green Press Initiative. The majority of our books are printed on Forest Stewardship Council (FSC)–certified paper, with nearly all containing 50–100 percent recycled content. The recycled fiber in our book paper is either unbleached or bleached using totally chlorine-free (TCF), processed chlorine-free (PCF), or enhanced elemental chlorine-free (EECF) processes.

More information about the Bank's environmental philosophy can be found at http://www.worldbank.org/corporateresponsibility.